A. J. O'Reilly

Alvira

The Heroine of Vesuvius

A. J. O'Reilly

Alvira
The Heroine of Vesuvius

ISBN/EAN: 9783337054854

Printed in Europe, USA, Canada, Australia, Japan

Cover: Foto ©ninafisch / pixelio.de

More available books at **www.hansebooks.com**

The Heroine of Vesuvius.

A REMARKABLE SENSATION OF THE SEVENTEENTH CENTURY.

FOUNDED ON FACTS RECORDED IN THE ACTS OF CANONIZATION OF ST. FRANCIS OF JEROME.

By REV. A. J. O'REILLY, D.D.,

Author of the "Martyrs of the Coliseum," "Victims of the Mamertine," "The Double Triumph," etc.

NEW YORK:

D. & J. SADLIER & CO.,

33 BARCLAY STREET AND 38 PARK PLACE.

Copyright,
D. & J. SADLIER & CO.,
1885.

INTRODUCTION.

THE PENITENT SAINTS.

The interesting and instructive character of this sensational narrative, which we cull from the traditions of a past generation, must cover the shortcomings of the pen that has labored to present it in an English dress.

We are aware that the propriety of drawing from the oblivion of forgotten literature such a story will be questioned. The decay of the chivalrous spirit of the middle ages, and the prudish, puritanical code of morality that has superseded the simple manners of our forefathers, render it hazardous to cast into the hands of the present generation the thrilling records of sin and repentance such as they were seen and recorded in days gone by. Yet in the midst of a literature professedly false, and which paints in fascinating colors the various phases of unrepented vice and crime, without the redeeming shadows of honor and Christian morality, our little volume must fall a welcome sunbeam. The strange career of our heroine constitutes a sensational biography charming and beautiful in the moral it presents.

The evils of mixed marriages, of secret societies, of intemperance, and the indulgence of self-love in ardent and enthusiastic youth, find here the record of their fatal influence on social life, reflected through the medium of historical facts. Therefore we present to the young a chapter of warning—a tale of the past with a deep moral for the present.

The circumstances of our tale are extraordinary. A young girl dresses in male attire, murders her father, becomes an officer in the army, goes through the horrors of a battle, and dies a *saint*.

Truly we have here matter sensational enough for the most exacting novelist; but we disclaim all effort to play upon the passions, or add another work of fiction to the mass of irreligious trash so powerful in the employ of the evil one for the seduction of youth. In the varied scenes of life there are many actions influenced by secret motives known only to the heart that harbors them. Not all are dishonorable. It takes a great deal of guilt to make a person as black as he is painted by his enemies. Many a brave heart has, under the garb of an impropriety, accomplished heroic acts of self-denial.

History is teeming with instances where the love of creatures, and even the holier and more sublime love of the Creator, have, in moments of enthusiasm, induced tender females to forget the weakness of their sex and successfully fulfil the spheres of manhood. These scenes, so censurable, are extraordinary more from the rarity of their occurrence than from the motives that inspire them, and thus our tale draws much of its thrilling interest from the unique character of its details.

"But what a saint!" we fancy we hear whispered by the fastidious and scrupulous into whose hands our little work may fall.

Introduction.

Inadvertently the thought will find a similar expression from the superficial reader; but if we consider a little, our heroine presents a career not more extraordinary than those that excite our surprise in the lives of the penitent saints venerated on the altars of the Church. Sanctity is not to be judged by antecedents. The soul crimsoned with guilt may, in the crucible of repentance, become white like the crystal snow before it touches the earth. This consoling thought is not a mere assertion, but a matter of faith confirmed by fact. There are as great names among the penitent saints of the Church as amongst the few brilliant stars whose baptismal innocence was never dimmed by any cloud.

Advance the rule that the early excesses of the penitent saints must debar them from the esteem their heroic repentance has won; then we must tear to pieces the consoling volumes of hagiology, we must drag down Paul, Peter, Augustine, Jerome, Magdalen, and a host of illustrious penitents from their thrones amidst the galaxy of the elect, and cast the thrilling records of their repentance into the oblivion their early career would seem to merit. If we are to have no saints but those of whom it is testified they never did a wrong act, then the catalogue of sanctity will be reduced to baptized infants who died before coming to the use of reason, and a few favored adults who could be counted on the fingers.

Is it not rather the spirit and practice of the Church to propose to her erring children the heroic example of souls who passed through the storms and trials of life, who had the same weaknesses to contend with, the same enemies to combat, as they have, whose triumph is her glory and her crown? The Catholic Church, which has so successfully promoted the civilization of society and the moral regeneration of nations, achieved her triumph by the conversion of those she first drew from darkness. Placed as lights on the rocks of eternity, and shining on us who are yet tossed about on the stormy sea of time, the penitent saints serve us as saving beacons to guide our course during the tempest. Many a feeble soul would have suffered shipwreck had it not taken refuge near those tutelary towers where are suspended the memorial deeds of the sainted heroes whose armor was sackcloth, whose watchword the sigh of repentance poured out in the lonely midnight.

While Augustine was struggling with the attractions of the world which had seduced his warm African heart, whose gilded chains seemed once so light, he animated himself to Christian courage by the examples of virtue which he had seen crowned in the Church triumphant.

"Canst thou not do," he said to himself, "what these have done? Timid youths and tender maidens have abandoned the deceitful joys of time for the imperishable goods of eternity; canst thou not do likewise? Were these lions, and art thou a timid deer?" Thus this illustrious penitent, who was one of the brightest lights of Christianity, has made known to us the triumph he gained in his internal struggles by the examples of his predecessors in the brave band of penitents who shed a luminous ray on the pitchy darkness of his path.

The life of St. Anthony, written by St. Athanasius, produced such a sensation in the Christian world that the desolate caverns of Thebais were not able to receive all who wished to imitate that holy solitary

Roman matrons were then seen to create for themselves a solitude in the heart of their luxurious capital; offices of the palace, bedizened in purple and gold, deserted the court, amid the rejoicings of a festival, for the date-tree and brackish rivulets of Upper Egypt!

Where, then, our error in drawing from the archives of the past another beautiful and thrilling tale of repentance which may fall with cheerful rays of encouragement on the soul engaged in the fierce combat with self?

To us the simple, touching story of Alvira has brought a charm and a balm. Seeking to impart to others its interest, its amusement, and its moral, we cast it afloat on the sea of literature, to meet, probably, a premature grave in this age of irreligion and presumptuous denial of the necessities of penance.

CONTENTS.

CHAPTER I.
Paris One Hundred and Fifty Years Ago, . PAGE 5

CHAPTER II.
The Usurer, ... 10

CHAPTER III.
A Mixed Marriage, ... 13

CHAPTER IV.
A Youth Trained in the Way he should Walk, . 18

CHAPTER V.
Our Heroines, ... 27

CHAPTER VI.
A Secret Revealed, ... 33

CHAPTER VII.
Tears on Earth, Joy in Heaven, . . . 42

Contents.

CHAPTER VIII.
Madeleine's Happy Death, ... 48

CHAPTER IX.
One Abyss Invokes Another, ... 52

CHAPTER X.
On the Trail, ... 57

CHAPTER XI.
The Flight, ... 62

CHAPTER XII.
Geneva, ... 71

CHAPTER XIII.
The Secret Societies, ... 75

CHAPTER XIV.
The Freemason's Home, ... 89

CHAPTER XV.
Tragedy in the Mountains, ... 96

CHAPTER XVI.
A Funeral in the Snow, ... 110

CHAPTER XVII.
An Unwritten Page, ... 115

Contents.

CHAPTER XVIII.
In Uniform, ... 125

CHAPTER XIX.
Remorse, ... 131

CHAPTER XX.
Naples, ... 141

CHAPTER XXI.
Engagement with Brigands, ... 147

CHAPTER XXII.
The Morning After the Battle, . . . 156

CHAPTER XXIII.
Return—A Triumph, ... 161

CHAPTER XXIV.
Alvira's Confession, ... 165

CHAPTER XXV.
Honor Saved, ... 183

CHAPTER XXVI.
Repentance, ... 190

CHAPTER XXVII.
The Privileges of Holy Souls, . . . 199

CHAPTER XXVIII.

A Vision of Purgatory—A Dear One Saved, . 202

CHAPTER XXIX.

Unexpected Meeting, ... 207

CHAPTER XXX.

Conclusion, ... 214

ALVIRA.

CHAPTER I.

PARIS ONE HUNDRED AND FIFTY YEARS AGO.

"Paris is on fire!" "The Tuileries burnt!" "The Hôtel de Ville in ashes!" There are few who do not remember how the world was electrified with the telegrams that a few years ago announced the destruction of the French capital. It was the tragic finale of a disastrous war between rival nations; yet the flames were not sent on high to the neutral heavens to be the beacon of triumph and revenge of a conquering army, but set on fire by its own people, who, in a fanaticism unequalled in the history of nations, would see their beautiful city a heap of ashes rather than a flourishing capital in the power of its rightful rulers. Fast were the devouring elements leaping through the palaces and superb public buildings of the city; the petroleum flames were ascending from basement to roof; streets were in sheets of fire; the charred beams were breaking; the walls fell with thundering crash—the empress city was indeed on fire. Like the winds unchained by the storm-god, the passions of men marked their accursed sweep over the fairest city of Europe in torrents of human blood and the wreck of material grandeur.

Those who have visited the superb queen of cities as she once flourished in our days could not, even in imagination, grasp the contrast between Paris of the present and the Paris of two hundred years ago. With a power more destructive than the petroleum of the Commune, we must, in thought, sweep away the Tuileries, the boulevards, the Opera-House and superb buildings that surround the Champs Elysées; on their site we must build old, tottering, ill-shaped houses, six and seven stories high, confining narrow and dirty streets that wind in lanes and alleys into serpentine labyrinths, reeking with filthy odors and noxious vapors. Fill those narrow streets with a lazy, ill-clad people—men in blouse and women in short skirts and clogs, squatting on the steps of antiquated cafés, smoking canes steeped in opium, awaiting the beck of some political firebrand to tear each other to pieces—and in this description you place before the mind's eye the city some writers have painted as the Paris of two hundred years ago.

But the old city has passed away. Like the fabulous creations we have read of in the tales of childhood, palaces, temples, boulevards, and theatres have sprung up on the site of the antiquated and labyrinthine city. Under the dynasty of the Napoleons the capital was rebuilt with lavish magnificence. Accustomed to gaze on the splendor of the sun, we seldom advert to its real magnificence in our universe; but pour its golden flood on the sightless eyeball, and all language would fail to tell the impression on the paralyzed soul. Thus, in a minor degree, the emigrant from the southern seas, who has been for years amongst the cabins on the outskirts of uncultivated plains, where cities were built of huts, where spireless churches of thatched roof served for the basilicas of divine worship, and where public justice was administered under canvas, is startled and delighted with the refinement and civilization of his more favored fellow-mortal who lives in the French capital.

Paris has been rudely disfigured in the fury of her Communist storm; yet, in the invincible energy of the French character, the people who paid to the conquering nation in fifteen months nine milliards of francs will restore the broken ornaments of the empress city. From the smoking walls and unsightly ruins of bureaux and palaces that wring a tear from the patriot, France will see life restored to the emblem of her greatness, that, phœnix-like, will rise on the horizon of time to claim for the future generation her position among the first-rate powers of Europe.

To the old city we must wend our way in thought. Crossing the venerable bridge at Notre Dame, we enter at once the Rue de Seine, where we pause before the bank and residence of Cassier

CHAPTER II.

THE USURER.

At a desk in the office we observe a low-sized, whiskered man. Intelligence beams from a lofty brow; sharp features and aquiline nose tell of Jewish character; his eye glistens and dulls as the heaving heart throbs with its tides of joy and sorrow. Speculation, that glides at times into golden dreams, brightens his whole features with a sunbeam of joy; but suddenly it is clouded. Some unseen intruder casts a baneful shadow on the ungrasped prize; the features of the usurer contract, the hand is clenched, the brow is wrinkled, and woe betide the luckless debtor whose misfortunes would lead him to the banker's bureau during the eclipse of his good-humor!

Cassier was a banker by name, but in

reality dealt in usurious loans, Shylock-like wringing the pound of flesh from the victims of his avarice. He was known and dreaded by all the honest tradesmen of the city; the curse of the orphan and the widow, whom he unfeelingly drove into the streets, followed in his path; the children stopped their games and hid until he passed. That repulsive character which haunts the evil-doers of society marked the aged ban er as an object of dread and scorn to his immediate neighbors.

In religion Cassier at first strongly advocated the principles of Lutheranism; but, as is ever the case with those set adrift on the sea of doubt, freed from the anchor of faith, the definite character of his belief was shipwrecked in a confusion of ideas. At length he lapsed into the negative deism of the French infidels, just then commencing to gain ground in France. He joined them in their secret gatherings, and joined them, too, in open blasphemies against God and plottings against the stability of the Government. The blood chills at reading some of the awful oaths administered to the partisans of those secret societies. They proposed to war against God, to sweep away all salutary checks against the indulgence of passion, to level the altar and the throne, and advocated the claims of those impious theories that in modern times have found their fullest development in Mormonism and Communism.

Further on we shall find this noxious weed, that flourishes in the vineyards whose hedges are broken down, producing its poisonous fruit. But it was at this period of our history that he became a frequent attendant at their reunions, returning at midnight, half intoxicated, to pour into the horrified ears of his wife and children the issue of the last blasphemous and revolutionary debate that marked the progress and development of their impious tendencies.

No wonder Heaven sent on the Cassier family the curse that forms the thrill of our tragic memoir.

CHAPTER III.

A MIXED MARRIAGE.

The Catholic Church has placed restrictions on unions that are not blessed by Heaven. Benedict XIV. has called them *detestable*. A sad experience has proved the wisdom of the warning. When the love that has existed in the blinding fervor of passion has subsided into the realities of every-day life, the bond of nuptial duty will be religion. But the conflict of religious sentiment produces a divided camp.

The offspring must of necessity be of negative faith. When intelligence dawns on the young soul, its first reasoning powers are caught in a dilemma. Reverential and filial awe chains the child to father and chains it to mother; but the father may sternly command the Methodist chapel for Sunday service; the mother will wish to see her little one worship before the altars of the Church. Fear or love wins the trusting child, but neither gains a sincere believer.

See that young mother, silent and fretful; the rouge that grief gives the moistened eye tells its own tale of secret weeping.

Trusting, confiding in the power of young love, attracted by the wealth. the family, or the manners of her suitor, she allows the indissoluble tie to bind her in unholy wedlock. Soon the faith she has trifled with assumes its mastery in her repentant heart, but liberty is gone; for the dream of conjugal bliss which dazzled when making her choice, she finds herself plunged for life into the most galling and irremediable of human sorrows—secret domestic persecution. Few brave the trial; the larger number go with the current to the greater evil of apostasy.

Cassier loved a beautiful Catholic girl named Madeleine. Blinded by the stronger passion, he waived religious prejudice. He wooed, he promised, he won. The timid Madeleine, beneath her rich suitor in position, dazzled by wealth, and decoyed by the fair promises that so often deceive the confiding character of girlhood, gave her hand and her heart to a destiny she soon learned to lament.

Fancy had built castles of future enjoyment; dress, ornament, and society waved their fascinating wings over her path. Unacquainted with their shadowy pleasures, her preparations for her nuptials were a dream of joy, too soon to be blasted with the realities of suffering that characterize the union not blessed by Heaven. Amid music and flowers, amid the congratulations of a thousand admiring friends, with heart and step as light as childhood, Madeleine, like victims, dressed in flowers and gold, led to the altar of Jupiter in the Capitol of old, was conducted from the bridal altar to the sacrifice of her future joy. Story oft told in the vicissitudes of betrayed innocence, and in the fate of those who build their happiness in the castles of fancy: like the brilliancy of sunset her moment of pleasure faded; the novelty and tinsel of her gilded home lost their charm, and the virtue of her childhood was wrecked on golden rocks. She no longer went to daily Mass; her visits to the convent became less frequent, her dress lighter; her conversation, toned by the ideas of pride and self-love reflected from the society she moved in, was profane and irreligious; and soon the roses of Christian virtue that bloom in the cheek of innocent maidenhood became sick and withered in the heated, feverish air of perverse influences that tainted her gilded home.

Sixteen years of sorrow and repentance had passed over Madeleine, and found her, at the commencement of our narrative, the victim of consumption and internal anguish, the more keen because the more secret. The outward world believed her happy; many silly maidens, in moments of vanity, deemed they could have gained heaven if they were possessed of Madeleine's wealth, her jewels, her carriages, her dresses; but were the veils that shroud the hypocrisy of human joy raised for the warning of the uninitiated, many a noble heart like Madeleine's would show the blight of disappointment, with the thorns thick and sharp under the flowers that are strewn on their path. The sympathy of manhood, ever flung around the couch of suffering beauty, must hover in sighs of regret over the ill-fated Madeleine, whose discolored eye and attenuated form, whose pallid cheek, furrowed by incessant tears, told the wreck of a beautiful girl sinking to an early tomb.

Her children—three in number—cause her deepest anxiety; they are the heroes of our tale, and must at once be introduced to the reader.

CHAPTER IV.

A YOUTH TRAINED IN THE WAY HE SHOULD WALK.

> To-morrow—
> 'Tis a period nowhere to be found
> In all the hoary registers of time,
> Unless, perchance, in the fool's calendar.
> Wisdom disdains the word, nor holds society
> With those who own it.
> 'Tis Fancy's child, and Folly is its father;
> Wrought of such stuff as dreams are, and as baseless
> As the fantastic visions of the evening.
> —COLTON.

LIKE one of those rare and beautiful flowers found on the mountain-side in fellowship with plants of inferior beauty, the heir of the Cassier family is a strange exception of heroic virtue in the midst of a school of seduction. The saints were ever exotics in their own circle. Their early histories are filled with sad records confirming the prophecy of our blessed Lord:

"The world will hate you because it loves not me."

The student of hagiology recalls with a sigh the touching fate of a Dympna who was the martyred victim of a father's impiety; of a Stanislaus pursued by brothers who thirsted for his blood; of a Damian who nearly starved under his stepfather's cruelty; of martyrs led to the criminal stone for decapitation by inhuman parents.

Louis Marie, the eldest of Cassier's children, was of a naturally good disposition. Through the solicitations of his mother and the guidance of an unseen Providence that watched over his youth, he was early sent to the care of the Jesuits. Under the direction of the holy and sainted members of this order he soon gave hope of a religious and virtuous manhood. Away from the scoffs of an unbelieving father and the weakening seductions of pleasure, he opened his generous soul to those salutary impressions of virtue which draw the soul to God and enable it to despise the frivolities of life.

The vacation, to other youths a time of pleasure, to Louis was tedious. Though passionately attached to his mother, yet the impious and often blasphemous remarks of his father chilled his heart; the levity with which his sisters ridiculed his piety was very disagreeable; hence, under the guidance of a supernatural call to grace, he longed to be back with the kind fathers, where the quiet joys of study and solitude far outweighed the short-lived excitement called pleasure by his worldly sisters. This religious tendency found at last its consummation in an act of heroic self-denial which leads us to scenes of touching interest on the threshold of this extraordinary historical drama.

At the time our narrative commences Louis was seriously meditating his flight from home and the world to bury himself in some cloister of religion. His studies of philosophy and history had convinced him of the immortality of the soul and the vanity of all human greatness. In his frequent meditations he became more and more attracted towards the only lasting, imperishable Good which the soul will one day find in its possession. "Made for God!" he would say to himself, "my soul is borne with an impetuous impulse towards him; like the dove sent from the ark, it floats over the vast waters, and seeks in vain a resting place for its wearied wing; it must return again to the ark."

The history of the great ones of the world produced a deep impression on Louis' mind. Emblazoned on the annals of the past he read the names of great men who played their part for a brief hour on the stage of life. They grasped for a moment the gilded bubble of wealth, of glory, and power; but scarcely had they raised the cup of joy to their lips when it was dashed from them by some stroke of misfortune or death. The pageant of pride, the tinsel of glory, were not more lasting than the fantastic castles that are built in the luminous clouds that hang around the sunset,

At college Louis was called on with his companions to write a thesis on the downfall of Marius. Nothing more congenial to his convictions or more encouraging to the deep resolution growing in his heart could be selected. The picture he drew from the sad history of the conqueror of the Cimbri was long remembered among his school companions.

Marius was seven times Consul of Rome; in the hapless day of his ascendancy he threatened to stain three-fourths of the empire with human blood. Blasted in his golden dream of ambition, driven into exile by victorious enemies, he was cast by a storm on the shores of Africa, homeless and friendless; in cold and hunger he sought shelter amidst the ruins of Carthage. Carthage, whose fallen towers lay in crumbling masses around him, was once the rival city of imperial Rome herself, and, under the able leadership of Hannibal, threatened to wrest from the queen of the Seven Hills the rule of the world. Now its streets are covered with grass; the wild scream of the bird of solitude and the moanings of the night-owl mingle with the sobs of a fallen demigod who once made the earth shake under his tyranny.

Louis read of the facts and sayings that doled out the sad tale of disappointment felt by those who seemed to possess all that the wildest ambition could dream of.

"Yesterday the world was not large enough for him," said a sage on the death of Alexander the Great; "to-day he is content with six feet of earth."

"What a miserable tomb is erected to the man that once had temples erected to his honor!" sighed a philosopher on viewing a mean monument on the sea-shore erected to the great Pompey, who could raise armies by stamping his feet.

"This is all the great Saladin brings to the grave," was announced by a courier who carried the great ruler's winding-sheet before him to the grave.

"Would I had been a poor lay brother," cried out the dying Philip II. of Spain, "washing the plates in some obscure monastery, rather than have borne the crown of Spain!"

That which took most effect on the mind of Louis was the eloquence of Ignatius when he met the young Xavier in the streets of Paris. "And then?" asked by another saint of an ambitious youth, did not lose its force with the holy youth who found himself, by some freak of blind fortune, heir to one of the millionaires of the French capital.

Louis, like St. Ignatius, would often stray to a shady corner of the garden, and there, with eyes fixed on the blue vault of heaven, he would sigh: "Oh! quam sordet tellus dum cœlum aspicio"—"How vile is earth whilst I look on heaven!"

One evening Louis had wandered into the garden to give full vent to a flood of thought that urged him on to give immediate answer to the calls of grace. God was pleased to pour additional light on his soul; and grace urged the immediate execution of his generous resolutions. That very morning the angry temper of his father and his bitter sarcasms against the faith Louis loved had embittered everything around his home. In tears, but with the fearless *abandon* of the true call, he resolved to quit his father's home that very night, and to break his purpose to his mother. She was the only one he really loved, and in wounding her tender heart was the hardest part of the sacrifice. In filial deference he prepared his mind to break the matter to his kind-hearted mother as gently as he could. He would submit the resolution to our Blessed Lord in the most Holy Sacrament.

Whilst going out to the venerable church of Notre Dame, a beautiful *calèche* is at the door, and two young girls, dressed in extravagant richness, are hurrying off to the fashionable rendezvous of the city; mildly refusing the invitation to accompany them, he hastens to accomplish the vows he has just taken before the altar.

Leaving Louis to his devotions, we pause to catch a glimpse of the lovely girls who seek happiness in another but less successful manner. The reader must know those interesting children bursting like fragrant flowers into the bloom of their maidenhood; they are the sisters of Louis, Alvira and Aloysia. Read those traits of innocence, of character, of future promise; treasure the beautiful picture for future reference; they are the heroines of our story.

CHAPTER V.

OUR HEROINES.

Alvira was tall for her age; she had a graceful, majestic carriage, and, although eminently handsome, there was a something in the tone of her voice and in the impression of her features that reflected a masculine firmness. Accomplished and intelligent, gay in society, and affable to all, she was a general favorite amongst her school companions. Yet she was at times of violent temper, and deep in the recesses of her heart there lurked the germs of the strongest passions. These passions, like lentils, grew with time and crept around that heart, until they concealed the noble trunk they clung to and made it their own. Alvira was often crimsoned with the blush of passion; a gentle rebuke or a contradiction was sufficient to fire the hidden mine and send to the countenance the flash of haughty indignation. Whilst yet in her maidenhood she longed for distinction. Fame leaped before her ardent imagination as a gilded bubble she loved to grasp. Tales of knight-errantry and chivalry were always in her hands, and bore their noxious fruit in the wild dreams of ambition they fired in the girl's mind. Often, when alone with her sister, with book closed in her hand and eye fixed on some article of furniture, her thoughts would be away winning crowns of fame on battle-fields of her own creation, urging on gallant knights to deeds of bravery, or arranging with humbled foes the terms of peace. She would start from her reverie with a sigh that told of the imprisonment of a bold, ambitious spirit that felt itself destined to wield a needle rather than a sword.

Aloysia is a sweet, blooming girl of fourteen. It often happens that fruits borne on the same stem are different in color and taste; so these two sisters were different in personal appearance and character.

Nature seems to have presided in a special manner over the moulding of Aloysia's exquisite frame. The symmetry of her person, hand and foot of charming delicacy, azure eye and rosy cheek, garlanded with nature's golden tresses, and the sweet expression of innocence in her features, would suggest her at once as a model for one of Raphael's Madonnas. Her disposition, too, comported with the beauty of her person. She loved retirement, and read only books of the noblest sentiment. The poets were familiar to her; she copied and committed to memory the passages of exquisite beauty. There was one feature in her character which bore a marked influence on her future destinies: it was her love for her sister.

We do not believe at all times in the genuineness of brotherly or sisterly love. Perhaps familiarity has deadened its keenness. Like the appreciation of the sunlight which rushes with thrilling force on the victim of blindness, separation or misfortune may rouse the dormant affection and prove its nobility and its power; but in our experience manifest fraternal charity is one of those things even the wise man knew to be rare under the sun. Where we have been privileged to look in behind the veil of the family circle, we are more convinced than ever that fraternal affection and all the boasted nobility of sisterly love dwindle down to a series of petty quarrels and jealousies as painful as they are unchristian and unbecoming. The reserve, or rather the hypocrisy of politeness, put on before strangers, is no criterion of the inward domestic life. Some one has said of ladies, "A point yielded or a pardon begged in public means so many hair-pullings behind the scenes." But this is too sweeping; there are noble, glorious exceptions in families where religion reigns, where fraternal charity finds a congenial soil; for it blooms in the fragrance of the other virtues, and is the first characteristic of a pious family. The world around are told to look for this as a sign by which they are to recognize the disciples of Him who loved so much.

Aloysia, in a true, genuine feeling of love, was bound in adamantine chains to her sister. Time and fortune, that shatter all human institutions and prove human feelings, consolidated the union of their hearts and their destinies. A stranger or stronger proof of the influence of sisterly affection could not be adduced; it dragged the beautiful, blushing Aloysia from the sphere of girlhood, to follow in the track of hypocrisy and of bloodshed so desperately trodden by her braver sister.

Our tale opens when the two girls had finished their education and were living in luxury and enjoyment. The days and hours passed merrily by. They would read in the shade, play and sing on the harp, would paint or work at wool, and in the afternoon, when the burning sun had left the world to the shade of evening, they would drive out in a magnificent *attelage* to the fashionable rendezvous of Paris.

Dream too bright to last! On the horizon is gathering the dark cloud that will dim the sunlight of their bliss, and cause them, in the dark and trying hour of trouble, to look back with the sigh of regret over the brilliant hours of youthful enjoyment.

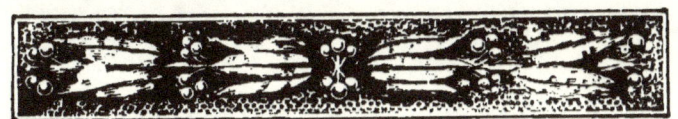

CHAPTER VI.

A SECRET REVEALED.

I thought to pass away before, and yet alive I am;
And in the fields all round I hear the bleating of
    the lamb.
How sadly, I remember, rose the morning of the
    year!
To die before the snow-drop came, and now the
    violet's here.

Oh! sweet is the new violet that comes beneath the
    skies
And sweeter is the young lamb's voice to me that
    cannot rise;
And sweet is all the land about, and all the flowers
    that blow;
And sweeter far is death than life to me that long
    to go.
                                    —*Tennyson.*

IT was a bright, cheerful morning in June. The sinking, feeble Madeleine had requested her domestics to carry her to the conservatory, that she might gaze again on the flowers that were soon to blossom on her grave. Death had lingered in his approach. The gay, the ambitious, and healthy he had taken all too soon; but for Madeleine, *who longed to go*, he tarried. Her little violets had already given their first fragrant kiss to breezes that passed with no mournful cadence through the cypresses of the lonely cemetery. Crumbling in her hand a faded rose, she breathed the thought so beautifully versified in after-times by the immortal bard of Erin:

> So soon may I follow
>   When friendships decay,
> And from love's shining circle
>   The gems drop away.
> When true hearts lie withered
>   And fond ones are flown,
> Oh! who would inhabit
>   This bleak world alone?

The sentiment was prophetic: other flowers of affection will be withered by the vicissitudes of destiny; fond ones will flee, leaving the world a wilderness for her last hours!

It often happens in the course of life that

we are driven by some inexplicable fatality to suffer those very afflictions we dread the most. We are told of persons who trembled for a lifetime at the horrid anticipation of being one day mad; it was the shadow of the judgment that was creeping on them, which cast them finally amongst the victims of the lunatic asylum. The suicide is the prophet of his own doom; the presentiment of death by drowning has but too often ended in a watery grave. Perhaps where the fibres of the heart are weakest, the strain brought on them by excited fancy snaps them in the misfortune that is dreaded; or perhaps some unseen spirit, charged with the decree of our individual sorrow, casts the dark shadow of his wing over our thoughts, and communicates the gloomy foreboding of a presentiment. The dying mother had one of these heart-tearing presentiments, so frequent and so mysterious in the history of human suffering.

She was guilty of a species of maternal idolatry: centred in her child Louis Marie, as rays gathered up into a focus, were all her hopes, her aspirations, her ideas of the future. If she could be assured she would live to see her son leading the armies of the empire, ruling in the cabinets of state, or worshipped in the circles of the great and learned, Heaven itself could not build up a greater joy in the limited horizon of her hopes; but an awful conviction crept over her that some misfortune would tear from her the object of her love like the fruit torn from the stem, like the young branch from the oak. In dreams she saw him struggling in the torrent which bore him away, or dragged to the hills at the feet of a wild horse. More than once she saw him on board a Government vessel, sailing with the hapless children of guilt to the convict settlements of southern seas —not as a felon, but an angel of light amongst the condemned.

Whilst Madeleine was sitting in the conservatory, musing over the gloomy anticipations her dreams had cast over her thoughts, Louis Marie came towards her.

A beam of joy lit up her hectic cheek; she impressed a kiss on the forehead of her darling son, and playfully reproved him for the dreams that gave her so much trouble.

"Mother," we fancy we hear Louis reply, "you would not surely give much credence to the imaginary evils of a dream. You know nothing can happen to us except by the arrangement of God; not even a hair can fall to the ground without his permission. I remember in college I was very much delighted with a thesis one of the fathers gave us on the Providence of God; it was so strange and so consoling to think that great Being who created so many millions of worlds, and keeps them flying around him with immense velocity, could occupy himself with us human beings, who are no more than insects moving on this world, which is but a speck in the immensity of the universe. But I know how it is—our souls are immortal, and hence we must soar higher than the countless worlds, were they ten times as great. Our blessed Lord, by coming amongst us and dying to save those souls, showed us that he thought more of us than of the bird of the air or the lily of the field, clothed in such charming magnificence. Is it unreasonable that, since he has given to each star a course, to each lily and each bird a time and a clime, he should also determine for us the course we should follow for his greater glory? And what, mother, if some unseen, invisible destiny should really call me away; if it were for the glory of God and the salvation of souls, would you not rejoice?"

Madeleine paused for a moment before venturing a reply. She trembled; a struggle between affection and duty passed within. Pleased with the rich flow of virtuous sentiment that made her still more proud of her child, she had caught the end of a golden thread and wished to unravel it further, but feared it would be snapped by some unpleasant discovery. Full of excitement, and her eyes fixed with a penetrating, enquiring gaze upon Louis, she answered:

"Louis, I should be false to the lessons I have endeavored to teach you in these last fleeting hours of my ill-spent life, were I not to rejoice in any destiny that would wrap up your future career in the glory of God; but I fear the enthusiasm of your young heart will misguide you. I know, from the serious tone of your voice and look in asking that question, you have been but feeling your way to make some crushing disclosure. I saw you crying in the garden this afternoon, and for some time past I have noticed a cloud of anxiety hanging over you. I had determined the first moment we were alone to know the cause of this trouble; and I now conjure you, by the affection and duty which you owe me as your mother, to let me share in your anxieties and in your councils."

Louis had really come to broach the terrible secret to his mother, but he had not yet courage; he struggled manfully to suppress internal emotions that might at any moment, like swollen rivers, overflow and betray their existence in a flood of tears Fearing to venture suddenly on the subject that was fullest in his heart, he partly evaded his mother's energetic appeal, and made such a reply as would elicit from her quick perception the declaration that trembled on his lips.

"If war were declared with our frontier foes, and our beloved King commanded the youth of the country to gird on the sword for our national defence, you, mother, would help me to buckle on mine?"

"Yes, Louis, I would give you proudly to the cause of France," continued Madeleine, feigning a patriotism she scarcely felt. "But, thanks be to God, I am not called on now to claim an honor that is at best a sacrifice and a calamity."

"But, mother, the war is declared, and I am to be a soldier in a sacred cause."

"How!" cried Madeleine excitedly. "The followers of the Black Prince again attacking us? The Turks seeking revenge for the defeat of Lepanto? or Christian Spain still intoxicated with its own dream of ambition? Whence come the sound of arms, Louis, to fire thy young ambition? If I judge rightly, thy disposition leads thee more to the cloister than to the battle-field."

" 'Tis so," replied Louis, who had adroitly brought the conversation to the subject that occupied his thoughts, and to the announcement that would ring with such thrill on his mother's ears. "And I am going to join a religious community immediately, to become a soldier in the great war of right against wrong—of this world against the next. To this war the trumpet-calls of grace have summoned me, and I come to ask the mother who would give me to the cause of my country to do the same for Almighty God."

A step was heard outside. Louis glided into the garden, and Madeleine was again found by her husband buried in tears.

CHAPTER VII.

TEARS ON EARTH, JOY IN HEAVEN.

MADELEINE, with all the keenness of her maternal heart, had caught the drift of Louis' mind, and felt the disclosure before it was made. A rough, rude remark from Cassier, and he left her to the silence and reflection she then vehemently desired. Reflection, in bringing before her a beautiful but sad picture, crumbled before her mental vision the castles that her affection and her hopes had built on the shadowy basis of Louis' future temporal glory. She felt, however, from the inspiration of faith a feeling of spiritual joy that he was called to the higher destiny of a favorite of Heaven. Had the fire of divine love glowed more fervently in her heart, she would feel the joy of ecstasy, such as consoled the death-bed of the mothers of the saints when the revelation of the sanctity of their children was the last crown of earthly joy. Anticipating the privilege the fond maternal heart would fain claim even in the kingdom free from all care, Madeleine often found herself contemplating her son fighting the brave fight, winning crown upon crown, and virtue flinging around him a shield more impenetrable than the fabulous Ægis of pagan mythology.

In the flippant boastings of Christian mothers there are many who pretend they have the fire of faith and divine love like the brave Machabean woman; but when the sore hour of real separation comes, the soft, loving heart bends and weeps. Nature, corrupt nature, resists the arrangements of God, and nature triumphs in the maternal tie. The spirit of Madeleine had made the sacrifice of her son, but the rude hand of nature swept the fibres of her heart and tore them asunder.

Night has gathered around the house of Cassier. Sleep has brought the silence of the tomb on the inmates. One alone is awake; gentle sobs tell of a heart struggling with its own desires, but a faint ray of moonlight shows him seeking strength on his knees before a crucifix.

Guide him, ye angels, in the sublime destiny to which Heaven calls! Treasure up those tears of affection; they are pearls for a crown in eternity! A long, farewell look at the old homestead, and Louis has fled.

In the night, when all were asleep, he stole down-stairs and into the silent street. The moon brightened the tears of his farewell; only his guardian angel saw, to register for his eternal crown, the inward struggle in which he had trampled on every tie of affection and pleasure. Disappearing in the narrow streets, he disappears also from the pages of our narrative until, in the extraordinary vicissitudes of time, he makes his appearance again in a scene both touching and edifying.

The morning dawn revealed the broken circle, the vacant chair in the family. Cassier was confused. Whilst others wept he moved about in deep thought. Stoic in his feelings and hardened in sympathies, he still felt all the tender anxieties of an affectionate parent. There are moments in the career of even the greatest sinners when sleeping conscience is roused to remorse. The shock the old man received in the loss of his amiable child opened his eyes to the unhappy state of his own soul; every act of ridicule he cast on the religious tendencies of Louis became arrows of memory to sting him with regret.

But these were transient moments of a better light. As meteors, darting across the sky, illumine for a few seconds the dark vault of heaven, and in the sudden exit of their brilliant flash seem to leave greater darkness in the night, thus the impulses of grace shot across the soul of Cassier; he struggled in the grasp of an unseen power, but suddenly lapsed into the awful callousness which characterizes the relapses of confirmed guilt; he pretended to smile at his weakness, and found a sorry relief in cursing and scoffing at everything the virtuous love.

Yet he offered immense rewards for information that would bring him in presence of the boy whose form he loved, but whose virtue he despised. Like the pagan persecutors of old, he vainly hoped, by fear or the tinsel of gold, to win back to the world and sin the magnanimous youth who had broken through the stronger argument of a mother's tears. Messengers were despatched in every direction; the police scoured the roads for miles outside the city; friends and acquaintances were warned not to harbor the truant.

A week passed, and no cheerful tidings came to lessen the gloom of bereavement. That Providence which made Louis a vessel of election had covered him with its protecting shield, and bore him like a vessel under propitious winds to the port of his destination.

In all the soft tenderness of girlhood the two sisters lamented their absconding brother. They, too, had been unkind to him. The sweet, patient smile that ever met their taunts, the mild reproof when they concealed his beads or prayer-book, his willingness to oblige on all occasions, were remembered with tears. When sitting by the mother's bed, the conversation invariably turned on Louis. In cruel fancy they deepened the real sorrow of separation by casting imaginary misfortunes on the track of the absent boy. One would sigh with the ominous *perhaps*.

"Poor Louis is now hungry!"

"Perhaps he is now lying sick and foot-sore on the side of some highway, without a friend, without money."

"Perhaps he has fallen in with robbers and is stripped of the few articles of dress he took with him."

"Perhaps he is now sorry for leaving us," sighed the tender-hearted Aloysia, "and would give the world to kiss again his poor sick mamma!"

But futile tears flowed with each surmise. No welcome messenger returned to bring tidings of the missing youth.

'Tis thus we love virtue; we sigh over departed worth when its brilliancy has faded from our sight.

CHAPTER VIII.

MADELEINE'S HAPPY DEATH.

Troubles, like migratory birds, never travel alone. As heavier billows cling together and roll in rapid succession and in thundering force on the rock-built barriers of nature, so the waves of trial and misfortune break on frail humanity in crushing proximity. The second and third billows of misfortune are fast undulating on the tide of time, and will sweep over the home of Cassier, leaving it a miserable wreck, a theme for the sympathy and the moral of a historian's pen.

The weakened, consumptive frame of Madeleine did not long survive the blow that Louis had prepared for her—not, indeed, in the sense of a guilty and blood-stained hand, but with the merit of an Abraham who, at the command of Heaven, prepared a funeral pyre for his child. Madeleine could scarcely weep; the grief of nature was calmed by the impulses of grace, and she felt in her heart a holy joy in the sublime destinies of her son. Could we, in the face of the holy teachings of the Church, institute a comparison between the mother of the soldier and the mother of the priest? Amidst sighs that were but the convulsive throes of a heart's emotion, she breathed often and aloud the *Deo gratias* of the faithful soul.

But like certain forces in nature that require but the slightest shock to give them irresistible power, by which they burst through their confining cells and set themselves free, the immortal spirit of Madeleine burst its prison cell and soared to its home beyond the skies.

We need not tarry over the painful, touching scene oft-told, and felt sooner or later in every home. Like snow disappearing under the sunshine, the life of Madeleine was fast melting away. At length, as if she knew when the absorbing heat would melt the last crystal of the vital principle, she summoned her family around her to wish them that last thrilling farewell which is never erased from the tablet of memory. In the farewell of the emigrant, torn by cruel fate from country and friends, hope smiles in his tears; the fortune that drives away can bring back; but the farewell of death leaves no fissure in its cloud for the gleam of hope—it is final, terrible, and, on this side the grave, irrevocable.

With faltering voice she doled out the last terrible warning that speaks so eloquently from the bed of death.

Whilst the aged priest recited the Litanies she raised her last, dying look towards heaven, and whispered loud enough to be heard, "O Mary! pray for my children."

Madeleine was no more. Her last sigh was a prayer that went like lightning to the throne of God from a repentant, reconciled spirit; at the same moment her liberated soul had travelled the vast gulf between time and eternity, and there, in the books held by the guardian angels of her children, she saw registered the answer to her prayer.

Madeleine was laid in a marble tomb amongst the first occupants of Père la Chaise. A small but artistic monument, still extant, and not far from the famous tomb of Abelard and Eloise, would point out to the curious or interested where sleeps among the great of the past the much-loved Madeleine Cassier.

> "God's peace be with her!" they did say,
> And laughed with their next breath.
> O busy world! how poor is thy display
> Of sympathy with death.

CHAPTER IX.

ONE ABYSS INVOKES ANOTHER.

In times gone by, in the so-called darkness of the Middle Ages, there were certain countries in Europe that believed in the existence of a fiend or ghoul that inhabited lonely places and unfrequented woods, and tore to pieces the imprudent traveller that ventured on its path. This fiend of the desert and lonely wood was at best but a fabrication of an excited fancy; it has long since passed away with the myths of the past, and exists only in the nursery rhymes of our literature. Yet in its place a malignant spirit of evil revels in the ruin of the human race; it delights in the crowd; it loves the gaslight, the lascivious song and wanton dance; it presides over our convivial banquets with brow crowned with ivy and faded roses;

whilst all the unholy delights of earth sacrifice to it, in return it scatters amongst its adorers all the ills and sorrows that flow from the curse of Eden, making a libation to the infernal gods of the honor, the fortune, and the lives of men. The ghoul or fiend of modern society is the demon of alcohol.

History records a remarkable victim in the ill-fated Cassier. When grief falls on the irreligious soul, it seeks relief in crime. The shadow of death that fell on his family circle, and the flight of his son in daring forgetfulness of his parental authority, which he had overrated, broke the last link of Christian forbearance in his unbelieving heart; when wearied of blaspheming the providence of God, he quaffed the fatal cup which hell gives as a balm to its sorrow-stricken votaries.

A cloud of oblivion must hide from the tender gaze of the young and innocent the harrowing scenes that brought misery on his home, ruin on his financial condition, and a deeper hue to the moral depravity of his blighted character,

One look of sympathy at our young heroines, and we will pass on to the thrilling course of events.

Like beautiful yachts on a stormy lake, without pilot, without hands to steady the white sail to catch the favorable wind, Alvira and Aloysia were tossed on a sea of trial which cast a baneful shadow over their future destinies. Tears had cast the halo of their own peculiar beauty over their delicate features; mourning and sombre costume wrapt around them the gravity of sorrow; and the adulation of a universal sympathy, pretended or real, supplied the attentions that flattered and pleased when they led the giddy world of fashion. The silence of grief hung around the magnificent saloons, once so gay; the wardrobe that contained the costly apparel, the casket that treasured the pearls o' Ceylon and gems of Golconda, were all closed and neglected. The treatment of their father was an agony of domestic trouble, in which they were tried as in a furnace.

A few weeks, however, and the darkest

hour of the storm had passed. Moments of relaxation brought beams of sunlight through the dissolving clouds; drives, walks, and even visits were gradually resumed.

A fit of illness brought Cassier to his senses. A forced abstinence for a few weeks saved him from the last and most terrible lot of confirmed drunkenness; but ruin was written with his own hand on the firm that made him wealthy. Quick-footed rumor, that hates the well-being of man, was abroad at its deadly work; public confidence in the bank began to wane, and each depositor lent the weight of his individual interest to accelerate the financial crash. The stone set in motion down the mountain assumes a force that no power could stay; on it will go until it rests in the plain. From the eminence of his boasted wealth the usurer found his turn come to whirl around on the wheel of fortune and yield to some other mortal, who is the toy of fortune, to grasp for a moment the golden key of avarice and ambition.

At length the crash has come. One of the largest depositors sends notice that in a week he will withdraw his funds.

Cassier saw ruin staring him in the face; when this sum was paid he would be a pauper. He would not dig, and in the pride of his heart he would not beg. Conscience, long seared in the path of impiety, has no voice to warn, no staff to strike. Cassier, wise in his generation of dishonesty, knows what he will do, and nerves himself for a desperate undertaking which leads us deeper and deeper into the history of crime, into the abysses of iniquity which invoke each other.

In a few days Paris is startled. Cassier has fled, and robbed his creditors of a million francs.

CHAPTER X.

ON THE TRAIL.

Evening had fallen over the city, and the busy turmoil of the streets had ceased; the laborer had repaired to his family, the wealthy had gone to their suburban villas, and licentious youth had sought the amusements over which darkness draws its veil. Politicians, newsmongers, and travellers made the café salons ring with their animated discussions. The policy of the Prime Minister, the probabilities of war, the royal sports of Versailles, and daring deeds of crime gathered from the police reports were inexhaustive topics for debate.

In one of the popular cafés there was a small gathering of men threatening vengeance on the delinquent Cassier; they had more or less suffered from his robbery, and they listened with avidity to every rumor that might lead to the probability of his capture. Amongst them there was an aged man of grayish beard, who was particularly loud and zealous in his condemnation of the dishonest banker. He railed against the Government, which, he said, was priest-ridden under the whip of Mazarin; the imbecility of the police; and the apathy of the citizens, who bore so peaceably such glaring acts of injustice and imposition. He poured out a volume of calumny against the priesthood, and blasphemed so as to cast a chill of terror through his less impious hearers.

He was suddenly stopped in his harangue by the entrance of a stranger in the coffee-room. He was a tall, thin man, wrapped in an over-cloak; he paced majestically across the room, and took a seat opposite the old man, who had suddenly become silent and was busily occupied reading the criminal bulletin. Over the edges of his paper the old man took a furtive glance at the stranger; their eyes met; a recognition followed, but as silent and as deep as with the criminal and the Masonic judge.

The old man rang the bell, and called for writing materials. He hastily scribbled a few words, closed, sealed the letter, then bade the waiter take it to his eldest son, who had retired to his apartments. He immediately took his hat and went out.

"Who is that old man?" asked the tall stranger, rising and advancing excitedly towards the waiter.

"That's Señor Pereira from Cadiz," retorted the waiter.

"Señor Pereira from Cadiz!" repeated the stranger. "No," he continued emphatically; "he is Señor Cassier from Paris."

"Cassier!" was muttered by the astounded debaters who had listened to the vituperative philippics of the Portuguese merchant.

"Cassier!" was echoed from the furthest end of the saloon, where some quiet and peaceful citizens were sipping their coffee and rum apart from the stormy politics of the centre-table.

Whilst an animated conversation was carried on two young lads came running down-stairs and rushed into the street through the front door.

"Who are those young men?" asked again the stranger of the waiter.

"They are the sons of Señor Pereira," was the answer.

"The sons of Pereira! They are the daughters of Cassier!" said the stranger in a loud voice, who had now become the hero of the room and had penetrated a deep and clever plot.

He ran to the street, but the fugitives had disappeared in the darkness; their gentle tread was not heard on the pavement, and no observer was near to indicate the course they had taken. The whole scheme of Cassier's bold disguise flashed with unerring conviction on the stranger's mind—the voice, the eye, the gait were Cassier's. He was familiar with the family, and in the hurried glance he got of the youths rushing by the saloon door he thought he recognized the contour of Alvira's beautiful face. He hastened to communicate his startling discovery to the Superintendent of the Police, and the city was once more in a state of excitement.

CHAPTER XI.

THE FLIGHT.

The sensation caused by the startling failure and embezzlement of the wealthy banker had scarcely subsided when the city rang with the news of his clever disguise and daring escape. Angry Justice, foiled in her revenge, lashed herself to rage, and moaned her defeat like the forest queen robbed of her young. The Government feared the popular cry, and proved its zeal by offering immense rewards for the arrest of the delinquent banker. The country around the city was guarded, every suspicious vehicle examined, and strangers ran the risk of being mobbed before they could prove their identity. False rumors now and then ran through the city, raising and quelling the passions like a tide. At one time the culprit is caught and safely lodged in the Bastile; at another he is as free as the deer on the plains. Cassier did escape, but some incidents of the chase were perilous and exciting.

Travelling in those days was slow and difficult. The giant steam-engines that now sweep over hills and torrents with a speed that rivals the swoop of the sea-bird were unknown. The rickety old diligence or stage-coach was only found on the principal thoroughfares between the large cities.

Cassier knew these roads would be the first taken in pursuit, and carefully avoided them. Seeking a destination where the chances of detection would be lessened, he was attracted towards Geneva, already famous as the hot-bed of secret societies and the rallying-point of infidelity. He would reach it by a circuitous route. From Paris to the historic old capital of Switzerland, in the centre of mountains and the heart of Europe, was a herculean journey for the fugitives.

On they went for two and three days' journey, stopping at humble inns on the roadside where the news of the capital had not reached. Time inured them to danger and calmed the fever of anxiety consequent upon their hurried and hazardous flight.

But the avenging law had followed in close pursuit. The officers of the Government were directed from village to village; they found themselves on the track of an old man and two beardless youths in naval cadet costume. The chase became exciting. Wealth and fame awaited their capture.

One evening, in the glow of a magnificent sunset, Cassier and his daughters were wending their way along one of the picturesque roads of the Côte d'Or. They were on the slope of a shady mountain, and through a vista of green foliage they could see the road they had passed for miles in the distance. The silence of the mountain-side was unbroken, save by the music of wild birds and the roar of a torrent that leaped through the moss-covered rocks towards the valley. The wild flowers gave aromatic sweetness to the mountain-breeze, and the orb of day, slowly sinking in a bank of luminous crimson clouds in the distant horizon, made the scene all that could be painted by the most brilliant fancy. Our young heroines gave frequent expression to their delight, but their aged sire was silent and watchful. He frequently took long and piercing looks on the road he had passed. Anxiety mantled on his wrinkled brow; a foreboding of danger cast its prophetic gloom over his spirits.

Suddenly he turned from a long, fixed look through the trees, and with a thrill of alarm cried out: "They are coming!"

For a moment he gave the jaded horses the whip. He refused any further information to the terrified girls; he bit his lip, drew his sword close to him, and prepared for a struggle; for he had resolved to die rather than go back a prisoner to Paris.

The pursuers were each moment gaining ground; the costume of the gendarmes was discernible as they galloped in a cloud of dust along the plain. The hill was long and heavy before the wearied horses of Cassier. He saw flight was vain; stratagem must come to his aid in the emergency.

At this moment he came to a turn in the mountain road where the trees were thicker and the shade more dense. Like a skilful general in the critical moment when victory and defeat hang, as it were, on the cast of a die, he conceived instantaneously the plan of a desperate expedient. He drew up his horses and bade his trembling children await his return.

Returning a few paces he secreted himself behind an oak-tree and calmly awaited the arrival of the Government officers.

Soon the clatter of the galloping horses was heard in the distance. The wild scream of startled birds resounded through the groves; the sun seemed to glow in a deeper crimson, the breezes sighed a mournful cadence through the waving foliage. On the troopers came up the side of the hill. Cassier has counted them—they are but two; despair has lent courage to his heart, and will give a giant stroke to his aged arm.

At the sight of the suspected *calèche* drawn up in the shady road, one of the pursuing officers gave spurs to his horse, and flew out before his companion to seize the prey—to be the first captor of the delinquent fugitive. Fatal indiscretion! Plunging along at desperate speed, and dreaming of gold and renown, the burnished sword of Cassier took his horse on the flank. Its rider fell to the earth; before he had seen his enemy, the sword of Cassier had pierced his heart.

A scream from the carriage announced that the scene had been witnessed by tender girls who had not been accustomed to deeds of violence and bloodshed. But the combat has now but commenced. The battle of the Horatii and Curatii, on which an empire depended, was not more fierce.

The second gendarme saw the fate of his companion; he reined his horse, dismounted, and came with drawn sword to meet the Parisian banker, who had now become a mountain bandit.

When Greek met Greek in the days of old, the earth trembled. Never was more equal or deadly fight. Cassier had learned the sword exercise in his youth as a useful art; the police officer was a swordsman from profession. For a moment sparks flew from the whirling, burnished blades. The silence of deep resolve wrapt the features of the combatants in fierce rigidity. Again and again they struck and parried, struck and parried, until wearied nature gave feeble response to the maddened soul. The aged Cassier felt, from his age and fatigue, about to succumb; gathering all his strength for a desperate effort, he threw his weight into a well-measured shoulder stroke, when, lo! his antagonist's sword flew in pieces—the brave gendarme fell weltering in the blood of his murdered companion.

All is still again. The sun has gone down in murky splendor, the birds are silent, and the solitude of the wild mountain-pass is like the night, that is darker after the flash of the meteor. The hapless but brave soldiers of justice lie in their armor on the field of battle; the fresh blood gurgles from the gaping wounds, and the madness of defeat is fiercely stamped on their bronzed features; one holds in deathgrasp the unsheathed sword he had not time to wield, the other still stares with open eye on the broken blade that proved his ruin.

A heavy splash and a crimson streak in the foam announce that the torrent has become the grave of the fallen police; the road, steeped with blood, is covered with fresh earth; the scene that witnessed the tragedy is fair and beautiful as before. Cassier, reassured, with bold step and pulse of pride, turns towards his conveyance to resume his journey.

Aloysia was just recovering from a fainting fit, and her sister had labored to restore her during the exciting moments of the deadly strife that had just been concluded. Neither of them saw the perilous situation of their father, and were thus saved the shock the extremity of his peril was calculated to have produced.

A few days found them safely across the frontiers of France, threading the passes of the Alps, and away from the grasp of justice, that pursued them in vain.

CHAPTER XII.

GENEVA.

As the wearied stag that has eluded the chasing dogs rests in safety in the covert of its native mountains, our fugitives at length breathed freely in the beautiful city of Geneva. Wild and grand as had been the scenery they passed through, the excitement of the flight and the fear of seizure had, to them, robbed nature of her charms. Ever and anon, indeed, they had looked around with searching eyes, but not to gaze in rapture on the snow-capped mountains, the green valleys, and crystal streams; it was rather to peer along the road they had passed, to see if any speck on the horizon would indicate the pursuing horses of the gendarmes. But now for the first time the magnificence of the Alpine scenery and the charm of the lovely queen of the Swiss valleys burst on their view. Mont Blanc, already seen from the north, seemed to lift its snowy drapery higher into the blue sky, and stood out more majestic in its crystallized peaks when seen from the bridges of the Rhone. Another firmament was seen through the clear, azure water of the beautiful lake; and although the air was cold and fresh in the icy chill of the mountains, and nature stripped of her green, yet our young heroines were charmed with their first view of the city, and rejoiced in the prospect of a long sojourn.

There are few spots in the world where the lovers of the sublimities of nature can drink in such visual feasts as at Geneva. Since railways have shortened distance and cut through mountains, there is no more fashionable rendezvous for the world of art than the suburbs of the Swiss capital. During the summer months every little nook on the surrounding mountain-sides is occupied by artists of every sex and of every nation. What juvenile album is complete without a sketch of Mont Blanc ? The old mountain stands out in its eternal majesty as a vision of awful beauty for old and young; and many a noble soul has been borne from the contemplation of the grandeur of nature to study in awe the greatness of Him " who makes mountains his footstools." The artificial beauties of the modern Geneva far surpass the old; yet those mountains, those peaks and snows and lakes, were always there. It was beautiful in the time of Cæsar; it was known to Constantine, and crept into importance and worth in proportion as science and art were developed in the civilization of Europe.

At the time we write the beautiful Swiss capital was one of the principal seats of learning in Europe. But, alas! its literature was blasted by the false principles of the Reformation. Like marble cenotaphs that have corruption within, Geneva, clothed with all the beauties of nature and art, was rotten to the core in her moral and religious character. She became the mother of heresiarchs, the theatre of infidelity, and by her press and preaching scattered far and wide the wildest theories of deism and unbelief. All the secret societies of the world were represented in her lodges, and within her walls were gathered men of desperate and socialistic politics who had sworn to overturn as far as they could the authority of society, to despise the rights of property, and to trample on the laws of order. There was no city in the world guilty of more blasphemy than this beautiful Geneva; and even to this day, as the sins of fathers descend to their children, the teachings of Calvin, of Bayle, and of Servetus hang like a chronic curse over the city to warp every noble feeling of Christian virtue.

Amongst the leaders of the secret societies, amongst the socialists who plot the ruin of their fellow-citizens, and amongst the infidels who blasphemously ridicule the mysteries of Christianity, we must now seek the unfortunate Cassier, who has arrived in Geneva.

CHAPTER XIII.

THE SECRET SOCIETIES.

To outsiders Masonry is a mystery. When Masons speak or write of themselves they give the world to understand they are but a harmless union for mutual benefit, and for the promotion of works of benevolence. That such is the belief of many individuals in the lower grades of Masonry, and even of some lodges amongst the thousands scattered over the face of the earth, we have no doubt; but that charity in its varied branches has been either the teaching or the fact amongst the great bulk of Freemasons during the last two hundred years we unhesitatingly deny.

In the ceremony of making a master-mason, and in a dark room, with a coffin in the centre covered with a pall, the brethren standing around in attitudes denoting grief and sorrow, the mysterious official who has the privilege of three stars before his name gives the aspirant this interesting history of the origin and aim of his office:

"Over the workmen who were building the temple erected by Solomon's orders there presided Adoniram. There were about 3,000 workmen. That each one might receive his due, Adoniram divided them into three classes—apprentices, fellow-craftsmen, and masters. He entrusted each class with a word, signs, and a grip by which they might be recognized. Each class was to preserve the greatest secrecy as to these signs and words. Three of the fellow-crafts, wishing to know the word of the master, and by that means obtain his salary, hid themselves in the temple, and each posted himself at a different gate. At the usual time when Adoniram came to shut the gates of the temple, the first of the three fellow-crafts met him, and demanded the word of the masters. Adoniram refused to give it, and received a violent blow with a stick on the head. He flies to another gate, is met, challenged, and treated in a similar manner by the second. Flying to the third door, he is killed by the fellow-craft posted there on his refusing to betray the word. His assassins bury him under a heap of ruins, and mark the spot with a branch of acacia.

"Adoniram's absence gives great uneasiness to Solomon and the masters. He is sought for everywhere; at length one of the masters discovers a corpse, and, taking it by the finger, the finger parts from the hand; he takes it by the wrist, and it parts from the arm; when the master, in astonishment, cries out '*Mac Benac*,' which the craft interprets by the words, 'The flesh parts from the bones.'"

The history finished, the adept is informed that the object of the degree which he has just received is to recover the word lost by the death of Adoniram, and to revenge this martyr of the Masonic secrecy.

Thousands of years have rolled over since the alleged death of the clerk of works at Solomon's temple, and if the streams of human blood that his would-be avengers have caused to flow have not satiated this blood-thirsty shade, those that Masons, Communists, Internationals, and other secret societies will yet cause to flow in the cities of Europe will surely avenge the ill-fated Adoniram.

It is also asserted by some Masons of strong powers of imagination that they take their origin from the Eleusinian Mysteries. These were pagan orgies attached to some Grecian temples. Surrounded by mysterious ceremonies and symbols, and supported by every mythical and allegorical illusion that could inspire awe or confidence, these mysteries were very popular amongst the Greeks.

"The mysteries of Eleusis," says the profound German mythologist, Creuzer, "did not only teach resignation, but, as we see by the verses of Homer to Ceres sung on those occasions, they afforded consoling promises of a better futurity. 'Happy is the mortal,' it is said there, 'who hath been able to contemplate these grand scenes! But he who hath not taken part in these holy ceremonies is for ever deprived of a like lot, even when death has drawn him down into its gloomy abodes.'"

Harmless and absurd as these mysteries were in the commencement, they afterwards lapsed into all the immoralities of pagan worship. But to give such a remote, and even such a noble, origin to the frivolous deism of modern Masonry is about as absurd as to say that men were at one time all monkeys.

The truth is, Freemasonry was never heard of until the latter part of the Middle Ages. It found its infancy among the works of the great cathedral of Strasburg. Erwin of Steinbach, the leading architect employed in the erection of this beautiful and stupendous work of architectural beauty, called around him other noted men from the different cities of Germany, Switzerland, and France; he formed the first lodge. The members became deputies for the formation of lodges in other cities, and thus in 1459 the heads of these lodges assembled at Ratisbon, and drew up their Act of Incorporation, which instituted in perpetuity the lodge of Strasburg as the chief lodge, and its president as the Grand Master of the Freemasons of Germany.

The masters, journeymen, and apprentices formed a corporation having special jurisdiction in different localities. In order not to be confounded with the vulgar mechanics who could only use the hammer and the trowel, the Freemasons invented signs of mutual recognition and certain ceremonies of initiation. A traditionary secret was handed down, revealed to the initiated, and that only according to the degrees they had attained. They adopted for symbols the square, the level, the compass, and the hammer. In some lodges and in higher grades (for they differ almost in every nation) we find the Bible, compass, and square only. By the Bible given to the aspirant he is to understand he is to acknowledge no other law but that of Adam

—the law which Almighty God had engraved on his heart, and which is called the law of nature (thereby rejecting the laws of the Church and society). The compass recalls to his mind that God is the central point of everything, from which everything is equally distant, and to which everything is equally near. By the square he is to learn that God made everything equal. The drift of these symbolic explanations is obvious.

In the ceremonies of initiation into the various degrees everything was devised that could strike the imagination, awaken curiosity, or excite terror. The awful oath that has been administered in some Continental lodges would send a thrill of horror through every right-minded person, whilst the lugubrious ceremonies the aspirant has to pass elicit a smile—such, for instance, of leading the young Mason with bandaged eyes around the inner temple, and in the higher grades presenting him with a dagger, which he is to plunge into a manikin stuffed with bladders full of blood, and declare that thus he will be avenged of the death of Adoniram! Then he is instructed in the code of secret signals by which he can recognize a brother on the street, on the bench, or on the field of battle. Carousing till midnight is a befitting finale to the proceedings of the lodge.

The doctrines or religious code of the Masons are, as their symbols indicate, deistic and anti-Christian. They openly shake off the control of all religion, and pretend to be in possession of a secret to make men better and happier than Christ, his apostles, and his Church have made them or can make them. "The pretension," says Professor Robertson, "is monstrous!"

How is this exoteric teaching consistent with the full and final revelation of divine truths? If in the deep midnight of heathenism the sage had been justified in seeking in the mysteries of Eleusis for a keener apprehension of the truths of primitive religion, how does this justify the Mason, in the midday effulgence of Christianity, in telling mankind he has a wonderful secret for advancing them in virtue and happiness —a secret unknown to the incarnate God, and to the Church with which he has promised the Paraclete should abide for ever? And even the Protestant, who rejects the teaching of that unerring Church, if he admits Christianity to be a final revelation, must scout the pretensions of a society that claims the possession of moral truths unknown to the Christian religion.

Whatever may have been the original cast of the religious views of the Masonic order, it is certain in its development it has become impious and blaspheming. In the latter part of the seventeenth century the Masonic lodges were the hot-beds of sedition and revolution; and long before the popes from their high watch-tower of the Vatican had hurled on these secret gatherings the anathema of condemnation, they were interdicted in England by the Government of Queen Elizabeth; they were checked in France by Louis XV. (1729); they were prescribed in Holland in 1735, and successively in Flanders, in Sweden, in Poland, in Spain, in Portugal, in Hungary, and in Switzerland. In Vienna, in 1743, a lodge was burst into by soldiers. The Freemasons had to give up their swords and were conducted to prison; but as there were personages of high rank among them, they were let free on parole and their assemblies finally prohibited. These facts prove there was something more than mutual benefit associations in Masonry. "When we consider," says M. Picot, "that Freemasonry was born with irreligion; that it grew up with it; that it has kept pace with its progress; that it has never pleased any men but those who were either impious or indifferent about religion; and that it has always been regarded with disfavor by zealous Catholics, we can only regard it as an institution bad in itself and dangerous in its effects."

Robinson of Edinburgh, who was a Protestant and at one time a Mason himself, says: "I believe no ordinary brother will say that the occupations of the lodges are anything better than frivolous, very frivolous indeed. The distribution of charity needs to be no secret, and it is but a small part of the employment of the meeting. Mere frivolity can never occupy men come to age, and accordingly we see in every part of Europe where Freemasonry has been established the lodges have become seed-beds of public mischief."

This was particularly true of the lodges of the central cities of Europe in the latter part of the seventeenth century. They were not only politically obnoxious to governments, but they became the agents and supporters of all the heretical theories of the day, and their evil effects were felt in the domestic circle. Like animals that hate the light and crawl out from their hiding-places when the world is abandoned by man, the members of those impious gatherings passed their nights in mysterious conclave. Fancy can paint the scene: weak-minded men of every shade of unbelief, men of dishonest and immoral sentiments, men who, if justice had her due, should have swung on the gallows or eked out a miserable existence in some criminal's cell, joined in league to trample on the laws and constitution of order, and, in the awful callousness of intoxication, uttering every blasphemous and improper thought the evil one could suggest. What must have been the character of the homes that received such men after their midnight revels? Many a happy household has been turned into grief through their demoralizing influence; mothers, wives, and daughters have often, in the lonely hours of midnight, sat up with a scanty light and a dying fire awaiting the late return of a son, a husband, or a brother; with many a sigh they would trace the ruin of their domestic felicity and the wreck of their family to some lodge of the secret societies.

Before appealing to facts and bringing the reader to a scene of domestic misery caused by those societies, we will conclude these remarks by quoting one or two verses from a parody on a very popular American song. We believe the lines representing the poor little child calling in the middle of the night, in the cold and wet, at the Masonic lodge for its father, to be as truthful in the realities of domestic suffering as they are beautiful and touching in poetic sentiment:

"Father, dear father, stop home with us, pray
    You never stop home with us now;
'Tis always the 'lodge' or 'lodge business,' you say
    That will not home pleasures allow.
Poor mother says benevolence is all very well,
    And your efforts would yield her delight,
If they did not take up so much of your time,
    And keep you from home every night.

"Father, dear father, stop home with us, pray!
    Poor mother's deserted, she said,
And she wept o'er your absence one night, till away
    From our home to your lodge-room I sped.
A man with a red collar came out and smiled,
    And patted my cheeks, cold and blue,
And I told him I was a good Templar's child,
    And was waiting, dear father, for you.

"Father, dear father, come home with me now;
    You left us before half-past seven,

Don't say you'll come soon, with a frown on your
    brow ;
'Twill soon, father dear, be eleven.
Your supper is cold, for the fire is quite dead,
    And mother to bed has gone, too ;
And these were the very last words that she said :
    ' I hate those Freemasons, I do ! ' "

CHAPTER XIV.

THE FREEMASON'S HOME.

LATE on a dark night in the commencement of November, wind and rain blowing with violence from the mountains, and the streets of Geneva abandoned, we find our young heroines sitting in a comfortable room. They are lounging on easy-chairs before a warm fire; the eldest is reading, and the youngest, although dressed in the pretty uniform of a naval cadet, is working at embroidery with colored wools.

Alvira and Aloysia, at the command of their father, have still preserved their disguise, at first irksome to their habits and delicacy of maidenhood; but necessity and fear toned down their objection, and they gradually accustomed themselves to the change. In girlish simplicity they were pleased with the novelty of their position.

They knew each other as Charles and Henry, and by these names we must now call them.

The old clock of the church on the hill sent the mournful tones of the eleventh hour over the silent city. Charles counted the solemn booms of the church bell, and then, as if resuming the conversation with Henry: "Eleven o'clock, and father not come home yet! I am sure I don't know what keeps father out every night so late; if poor mother were alive, she would never stand this."

"But perhaps pa may have important business and can't come home," we hear the amiable Henry suggesting.

"Business! Nothing of the kind. He has got in amongst some old fools who pretend to have more knowledge than their grandfathers, and are deceiving old women of both sexes to such a degree that they actually fancy they are inspired to make new Bibles, new commandments, and new churches."

"But father may be trying to put them

right," replied Henry softly, "and perhaps feels as you do. How sad to see them going astray!"

"No," answered the other with greater animation, "he is as bad as any of them. You remember long ago how he used to make poor mother cry when speaking of the great mystery of the Redemption; he called it the greatest swindle the world ever saw. You remember what blasphemous and insulting language he addressed to the Sisters of St. Vincent when they asked for alms in honor of the Blessed Virgin; and you know how he is always reading the most impious works.

"He is now shut up in one of those myserious rooms called Freemason lodges, where, if report be true, the enemies of Church and state plot the ruin of mankind. Henry, he is not only an infidel and a Freemason, but he is unkind to us."

Saying these last words, Charles rose and paced up and down the room, as if full of passion.

Faith, like anemones that flourish in the

depths of the ocean when the surface is tossed with storm, was concealed in the heart of Charles, and inspired those feelings of holy indignation which live in secret in the heart even when passion rages in triumph without.

Henry ventured a reply, but the excited manner of her sister checked her, and, burying her face in her hands, she remained in silence. Well she knew Charles was right, and in the deep sympathy of her innocent, loving heart her feelings crept into prayer for her erring parent, and silent tears suffused her eyes.

Whilst the two girls were thus engaged —the one pacing the room and biting her lips with annoyance, the other wrapt in prayer and tears—the step of Cassier was heard on the stairs.

It was unfortunate for Charles. He had given loose rein to his passion, and it was at this moment beyond control. The scene reminds us of a poor wife, the hapless victim of a drunkard's home, drawing on herself brutal treatment, when, in the lonely hours of midnight and in the pent-up feelings of a breaking heart, she would incautiously reprove the maddened wretch who is reeling home to her under the fumes of intoxication; thus Charles gave vent to feelings she had long nursed in her bosom, and spoke in disrespectful language of reproof to her intoxicated father.

Cassier had come from the carousals of the lodge. The fumes of the old wines had reached his brain; the fearless and unexpected reproof of Charles startled him. In an instant the demon of intemperance reigned in his heart; without waiting to answer, he approached the girl, gave her a severe slap on the face, and ordered her to her apartments.

Charles and Henry retired to a sleepless couch, and their pillow was moistened with many bitter tears before the dawn of the morning.

In a small spark commences the conflagration that destroys cities; the broad river that flows with irresistible majesty through our plains commences in a rivulet leaping and sparkling on the green hill-side; the mighty avalanche that sweeps with the roar of thunder through the Alpine ravines commences in a handful of loosened snow. Thus to a thought, a guilty desire uncontrolled, may be traced the greatest moral catastrophes.

A cloud passed over the thoughts of Charles. From the momentous evening she received the rebuke of her father, her heart became the battle-field of contending emotions. She brooded in silence over imaginary wrongs, and thus gave to a latent passion the first impulse that led to disastrous consequences. Diseased fancy lent a charm to thoughts long forgotten, and recalled the pictures of pride and ambition that had so often gilded the horizon of her young hopes. To be free and have wealth, she thought, was worth swimming across a river of blood to gain.

A temptation seized the thoughts of Charles. It clung to her like the bloodsucker drawing fresh streams from young veins. Notwithstanding her efforts to shake off the terrible temptation, and because she did not seek aid in the sacraments of the Church, it lived and haunted her in spite of her will. We tremble to write it —'twas to murder her father.

CHAPTER XV.

TRAGEDY IN THE MOUNTAINS.

> Come, you spirits
> That tend on mortal thoughts, unsex me here,
> And fill me from the crown to the toe topful
> Of direst cruelty! Make thick my blood;
> Stop up the access and passage to remorse,
> That no compunctious visitings of nature
> Shake my fell purpose, nor keep peace between
> The effect and it. Come to my woman's breasts,
> And take my milk for gall, you murdering ministers,
> Wherever in your sightless substances
> You wait on nature's mischief! Come, thick night,
> And pall thee in the dunnest smoke of hell,
> That my keen knife see not the wound it makes,
> Nor heaven peep through the blanket of the dark,
> To cry, "Hold, hold!"
> —MACBETH.

Poor Alvira! Her morning dawned after a restless, sleepless night. Phantoms of terror haunted her couch. The agonies of anticipated remorse had cast a withering shadow on her thoughts. She could not believe her own depravity in entertaining for a moment such a thrilling temptation.

Was it a dream? Was it the hallucination of a spirit of evil that revels in the human passions? "I, who love my father notwithstanding his faults, who would tremble at the gaze of my mother looking down from heaven on my awful impiety, and would hear from her tomb her scream of terror, her curse of vengeance on my parricidal guilt—could I be the foolish wretch that would consent to a deed of crime which would make me a fugitive from the face of men, and haunt my rest with the ghost of a murdered father?"

Thus Alvira mused. But a demon laughed at her tender conscience; deep in hell they had forged a terrible temptation. They knew the walls of the citadel of morality, built alone on natural virtue and unaided by divine grace, would soon crumble before their powerful machinations. In moments of sober reflection our resolutions are like prisms of basalt, that will not be riven by the lightning, but which in the hour of real trial prove to be ice-crystals that a sunbeam can dissolve. The powers that wage war with frail humanity have hung on the portals of the infernal kingdom, as trophies of triumph over man and insult to God, the resolutions of mortals made in moments of fervor and broken in weakness.

Days roll on; they bring their sunshine and clouds, but no change in the unhappy family; a change there was for the worse in the appalling development of the infidel and socialistic tendencies of their impious father. His language, less guarded, seemed to teem with new insults against religion and God, and contributed to confirm the chill of horror with which he was met by hapless children that sighed over the loss of filial love. His late returns from the lodge, and occasionally those sad ebullitions of intemperance, continued to be their deep affliction.

In proportion as love twines itself around the heart it absorbs all other feelings, it draws the passions like lentils around itself; so the contrary feeling of hatred, when permitted to enter the sanctuary of the heart, assumes at once a tyrannical sway, whose wicked demands of gratification become more and more imperious and exacting day by day, and rears a throne that becomes impregnable in proportion as the sun is allowed to set on its possessions. Even filial love has withered under the shadow of Cassier's worthlessness.

In lonely walks along the lake, in conversations, and in tears the two girls lamented their fate. The beauty of virtue withered within their bosoms. They resembled two beautiful flowers torn from their bed, and cast with the weeds of the garden to taint in their decay the breezes they would sweeten if left on their stem. They longed for the pleasures that pleased in the day of prosperity; the dance, the banquet, and those visits that won the momentary gratification of flattery and admiration were sighed for. So irksome was the monotony and so uncongenial the rôle forced upon them by disguise, they hailed with joy the least circumstance that might be the harbinger of a change.

It is at hand. Once more the excitement of chase! The vigilance of their astute father has placed them again in the *calèche*, and spirited horses are galloping from the Swiss capital.

News from Paris has arrived; the failure, the flight, the reward, are passed around in a sensational romance, and the disappearance of two police officers lends the charms of mystery to the embellished rumor. Cassier—the hero of the tale, the unsuspected guilty one—went around and told the news with all the sanctimonious whining and eye-uplifting of a ranting preacher. In the meantime he matured his plans, and before suspicion could point her finger at him he fled to another retreat to elude for a while the justice of man to meet his awful doom from the hands of God.

During the night Cassier and his children ascend the terrific pass of the Tête Noir; he proposes to hide from the threatened storm in the cloister of Martigny. This is a venerable Benedictine monastery, erected in the eleventh century by a Catholic prince, under the sanction of Urban II., possessing, besides many other privileges, that of sanctuary for fugitive prisoners.

The dangers of the road and the fear of pursuit lent additional terror to the wild mountain scenery; at one moment they are dizzy looking into awful chasms formed by huge perpendicular rocks; then the overhanging cliffs would seem every moment to break from their frail support and rush down the steep mountain in an avalanche of stone. In cold that penetrated to the very bones, amidst the roar of torrents leaping through caverns of ice, and in dangers unseen and therefore more dreadful, they passed a restless journey through the mountains, and arrived at the charming village of Martigny, over which the monastery presided like the fortress of a mediæval castle protecting the feudal territory of the petty ruler. Wearied, but pleased at the novel situation into which chance had cast them, Charles and Henry approached the venerable pile with feelings of reverence they had never felt. The silence of the tomb reigned around, and the old gate was closed. Whilst wondering how men could come voluntarily to live in such a solitude, and how they got the necessaries of life, a bell tolled solemnly from one of the towers; its soft, mellow tones rolled in sweet echoes across the mountains. Immediately the place became thronged with men in the habit of the Benedictine Order, hastening to and fro to commence their daily work. An aged porter bowed the strangers into a neat apartment, and summoned the Superior. No questions were asked, but comfortable rooms were appointed to them, and they were conducted in silence to the refectory, where a plain but substantial meal was placed before them. Thus commenced a visit the most extraordinary in the records of this venerable mountain cloister.

Charles and Henry were charmed with everything, although they found themselves in strange contrast with desires of worldly pleasure they had recently entertained. The wild, rugged scenery, the solemn silence of the house, and the sanctity of the mortified monks made a deep and solemn impression on the tender hearts of the young visitors, who felt the delicacy of their position in enjoying a forbidden hospitality. The example of the evangelical perfection practised by these holy servants of God insensibly drew Charles and Henry to love the sublime virtues they practised. Nothing impressed them more than the solemn chant of the Office at midnight. The slow, solemn enunciation of each word by a choir of hoary anchorets rolled in majestic cadence through the precipices of the mountains, and died away in the distant ravines in echoes of heavenly harmony.

An aged father was appointed to entertain the strangers. He led them to points on the mountain where the view was most enchanting; skilled in ancient monastic lore, he entertained them with anecdotes and histories from which he drew the most instructive morals. One cheerful afternoon, when seated on the rocks viewing a magnificent sunset, the aged monk told them his own history. He had been a soldier of fortune. In youth his ambition was as boundless as the horizon; he worshipped his sword and loved the terrors of battle. Fortune smiled on his hopes, and he moved on from grade to grade, until he became commander of a division.

He was present at the fatal field of Salzbach, where the great General Turenne fell in the commencement of the battle. The aged warrior, forgetting the gravity of his years and his habit, would speak in the fire of other days, suiting his action to the word,

He told his listeners the touching tale of his conversion. The death of the beloved Turenne, and at the same time the demise of his mother, made him enter seriously into self, repeating the farewell words of a celebrated courtier who left the French court to don the habit: "Some time of preparation should pass between the life of a soldier and his grave." He heard the great St. Vincent de Paul preaching on the vanities of life; his resolutions were confirmed, and tears started to his eyes as he recounted how happy he was in his home in the cliffs and the clouds.

Charles loved to hear the aged man's reminiscences of his military career. Fired with chivalrous aspirations, she could spend a lifetime in the regions of fancy so fervidly depicted from their Alpine retreat. Poor Aloysia was attracted to the higher and more real glories of the virtuous lives of those holy men. She felt she could stay with them for ever; and there, in the secrecy of her own heart, and before the altar of our Holy Mother, she made promises that shared in the merits of vows. When free, she would give herself to the love of God and the preparation for eternity in some secluded retreat of religion and virginity.

But the nearer the altar, the further from God. Reverse the picture, and another scene must be contemplated. Is it the venerable cloister buried in the snow, buffeted by the storm, and threatened by the avalanche? Is it the awful death of starvation hanging in all its gloomy anticipations over the community isolated by the snow-storm from the civilized world around? Or will it be the just indignation of the holy monks in finding the true character of the refugees whom they have sheltered in ignorance, contrary to the canons of the Church? Or will the still more devastating and ruthless storm of religious persecution seek the sanctuary in the clouds to desecrate it, to scatter its inmates and wreck its cloisters?

A calamity as thrilling and not less anticipated will fling a sad memory around the venerable cloisters of Martigny.

Cassier is in the group listening to the aged monk recount his adventures; with knitted eyebrows he hears him moralizing on the awful destiny of the future. He is a silent listener; the conversation is carried on by the garrulous and interested youths and the happy, virtuous old monk. A forced sobriety, or the atmosphere of virtue which he dreads, has cast a gloom over him. His thoughts are still reeking with the blasphemy of the Masonic lodges, and, though restrained by politeness from intruding his unbelief, he expresses in scowls and monosyllables his dissentient feelings.

Charles still burns with indignation at her father's irreligion and personal ill-treatment. Her flushed countenance and agitated manner were at times indexes of passion, revenge, and self-love; for a moment the feeling is strong and irresistible, then calms again with the holier sentiments of remorse and self-condemnation.

A morning as brilliant as ever lit up the glaciers of Mt. Blanc rose over the cloisters. Charles and Henry accompany their father on a stroll through the mountain. They miss their kind Mentor, who is on a retreat for some days. Henry, commencing to love solitude, strays from her father and Charles to gather ferns and wild flowers creeping from the crevices of the rocks, or rising with exquisite beauty from a layer of snow. They are emblems of her own innocence and fragrant as her virtue, growing in the wilderness and shedding their charms on rocks and snow-peaks, instead of ornamenting gardens of culture and beauty. Poor Aloysia would be more at home in some arbor of innocence where angels love to tarry, and where the voice and gaze of the worldly-minded have never fallen.

Cassier and Charles had slowly climbed to a projecting rock where nature had made a large table covered with grass. On one side the ascent was easy, but the other overhung a frightful precipice. They had entered into an animated conversation;

Aloysia, down beneath, could hear the sharp, quick answers of Charles, but, as such was usual in the temper of Charles, she did not notice it.

But lo! another moment, and a wild, shrill scream bade her look up; her father was no longer on the ledge of rock, and Charles flung her arms towards heaven and fell in a swoon on the edge of the precipice.

CHAPTER XVI.

A FUNERAL IN THE SNOW.

WHEN Charles had recovered her consciousness, she found herself reclining on the lap of Henry, who had been bathing her face with snow and tears. A long, painful call of her name had reached the inmost recess of her being whither consciousness had repaired. Springing to her feet, startled as if from a frightful dream, she gazed around. Memory and sight returned; folding her face in her hands, she cried in a paroxysm of grief: "My God! what have I done?"

This was the only intimation she ever gave Aloysia that in the heat of passion she had pushed her father over the precipice; she was his murderer. In their conversation the old man, more, perhaps, through impiety than conviction, misrepresented the good monks. We will not reproduce the stereotyped calumnies that even nowadays unbelievers love to heap upon the religious communities of the Catholic Church. The madness of passion took control in the breast of Charles. Scarcely knowing what she did, she pushed her aged father towards the precipice; he slipped, fell over into the chasm, and passed into eternity with blasphemy on his guilty lips.

The two sisters wept together for hours. Innocence, guilt, and retribution blended together in a scene of awful tragedy amid the glaciers of Mt. Blanc.

Seldom in the deeds of brigandage, in crimes committed in dark caves and lonely mountain paths, was there perpetrated a fouler murder; seldom in the sensational records of human depravity do we find the desperado of parricidal guilt under the delicate frame of girlhood. Yet was she rather an instrument in the hands of avenging Heaven than a monster of moral iniquity. At that moment the cup of iniquity was full for the wretch who had long tested the mercy of God. That Providence which blinded the Jews in judgment for ingratitude, and made them the instruments for the fulfilment of eternal decrees of redemption, withdrew from Alvira the protection that made her, whilst she accepted the guilt, the instrument of judgment.

Rising to her feet with a sense of her desperate condition, making a few hurried explanations how her father slipped and lost his balance, she approached tremblingly the fatal edge. Leaning over, she saw the corpse of her father lying in a pool of blood in the deep chasm below. The scene of that sad moment was indelibly impressed on her memory, and in after-hours of remorse haunted her with its horrors.

With nerve and courage, called forth by the awful circumstances of the moment, they descended the mountain to the foot of the ravine where the body lay in the snow.

The descent was steep and treacherous, and guilty conscience made Charles tremble lest at any moment she would lose footing and be precipitated down the dark and gaping chasms formed by glaciers and rocks. After hours of toil, and with imminent peril, they found the body of Cassier. A dark pallor had clouded his features, a ghastly stare, closed teeth, and a clenched hand bespoke the last sentiment of human passion. Alvira trembled and stood powerless for a few moments. Still, necessity nerved her to action. She removed the money and valuables from the body of her father, and, in the midst of wailings that echoed mournfully through the lonely mountain, they made a grave in the snow. Wrapping him in his cloak, they laid him in a bank of soft crystals through which the blood had trickled in crimson streams.

Thrilling and sad for Aloysia and Alvira the last moments of this funeral ceremony. Gently they placed the cold snow on the remains of their father. The wild eagle swooped around in anger, and the wind swept with ominous sighs through deep ravines of the rugged mountain. The gigantic cliff over which Cassier had been hurled by his maddened child frowned over them in awful majesty. It would be in centuries to come the cenotaph of a dishonored tomb. The winter would come again with fresh snow to cover this valley of death; the sun would pour its cold rays on the frozen mound that marked the grave of Cassier. No tear of affection would moisten the icy shroud, but, in sympathy for the hapless child stained with his blood, whose crime was condoned in the provocation caused, the world has cast its abhorrent curse on the grave of the reprobate.

> "There let every noxious thing
> Trail its filth and fix its sting;
> In his ears and eyeballs tingling,
> With his blood their poison mingling,
> Till beneath the solar fires,
> Rankling all, the curse expires."

CHAPTER XVII.

AN UNWRITTEN PAGE.

The noise of life can ne'er so dull our ear,
  Nor passion's waves, though in their wildest mood,
That oft above their surge we should not hear
  The solemn voices of the great and good.

As oft in icicles a flower remaineth
  Unwithered until spring its buds unchain,
The young heart through life's change a good re-
    taineth,
  And will exhume its summer leaves again.

WHEN Charles and Henry had breathed their last sigh over the snowy mound that covered the earthly remains of the hapless Cassier, they continued their descent down the mountain. They dared not go back to the cloister; they fled when no one pursued, for outraged conscience is its own avenger. Each stir in the brushwood, a loosened stone rolling quickly by, or the fluttering and scream of startled birds of the solitude, made them tremble.

Night was fast coming on; the sharp peaks of the Tête Noir were dimmed with clouds, and frowned with ominous terror on the path of the terrified fugitives. Through dangers of every kind, with bruises and wounds all over their delicate frames, they reached in the night the beautiful village of Chamounix. Refreshed with sleep and food, they prepared themselves for their future course, which for a while will be perilous, sensational, and extraordinary.

Free from the control of an intemperate and tyrannical father, possessing immense wealth, they cast themselves into a whirlpool of deceitful pleasure, and for a while, in yielding to the longings of misguided youth, hushed the qualms of conscience, which can only rest in the bosom of virtue.

Once more free, the thought naturally came of returning to the dress that became their sex. Aloysia, whose sense of delicacy was still as tender as the sensitive plant yielding to human touch, pleaded in tears for a return to the simple ways of girlhood, to the life and society more congenial to their habits and more in keeping with the laws of God and of nature. Alvira had yielded for a moment. But the love of travel, which in those days could not be gratified in their true condition of young and handsome girls without guardians, whilst in their male disguise not a shadow of suspicion or impropriety would interfere with them; the novelty of their condition, assuming each day some new attractions; the curiosity innate in the feminine breast to hear and see things outside her own circle; above all the hallucinations flung on the path of disguise by the fiend of evil, who thus intrigued for the final ruin of his unsuspecting victims, made them agree mutually to pass a short time in travelling around as naval cadets; then, tired and surfeited with their triumph over nature, they hoped to retire into the sphere of utility destined for them by Providence.

But, to our own and to our readers' regret, we must pause in our biography. The sources from which we cull these interesting details have cast historic silence over our heroines' ramblings of three years. What a volume of sensation they suggest! Were we given to the doubtful utility of fictional biography, were we weak enough to enrich ourselves by pandering to the morbid and often depraved longings of modern literary taste, we might fill a couple of volumes with scenes of excitement, of "hair-breadth 'scapes," and the heart-palpitating suspenses of misplaced love. We could not draw a picture more interesting or strange than those two sweet maidens in their disguise. We see them in the salons of the wealthy, in the clubs of the politicians, and at the billiard-tables of giddy youth who little dream of the intrusion, which, if they understood, would make them more happy. We fancy we see those youths, so polished, so gay, and withal so handsome, the idols of the society they move in; we hear compliments about those delicate hands, those small feet, those charming eyes.

Our sympathy would chronicle the sad fate of many an unsuspecting maiden who loved and pined in the dream of secret love towards the young officers that had crossed their path, whilst they revelled in cruel delight in their triumph over their own frail, tender-hearted sex. Our tale might unravel the plottings of hopeful mothers who vainly plied the utmost worldly ingenuity to gain for their daughters already passed the meridian of youth such promising and charming husbands. What skill it would demand to describe the chagrin of those old and young ladies, if they discovered the fraud which so heartlessly trifled with the sacred feeling of love!

We will not tarry over imaginary incidents whilst terrible and thrilling scenes are before us. The record of those extraordinary maidens is only now commencing in all its romantic attraction. It is not the vicissitudes of an erring life that inspire our pen in this brief sketch, but the merciful designs of Providence in following and wresting from perdition a noble soul, endeared to heaven by the prayers of a repentant mother, by the sighs of a saintly religious, and by its own love for the immaculate Queen of Heaven.

Alvira opens her soul to the impulses of grace, but in dangerous and guilty procrastination she passes through some startling vicissitudes before the Almighty, impatient as it were for her love, draws her to him by one of the most touching miracles recorded in the wonders of hagiology. We will hurry on to those events, which will warm our hearts with love towards God, and make us look up with a deep feeling of awe towards that "mercy which is above all his works."

Three years of strange vicissitude rolled over the career of our heroines. Some thousands of pounds gilded the path they passed over. With all the recklessness of youth, they squandered their ill-gotten money. Many a poor ruined family eked out a miserable existence, whilst their gold, entrusted to the wretched banker who had gone to his account, was flung recklessly on the tables of chance by the children he had nursed in the school of iniquity. Like sand passing through the fingers, like corn through the perforated sack, their thousands dwindled away, giving place to the bitter hour of retaliation, of punishment, which will yet come for those hapless children of folly.

It did not please Almighty God to hurry them to a dreadful judgment by sudden or awful death. He has other and even keener pangs than those of death, but they come rather from the hand of mercy than of justice. They are the pangs of remorse, which tear the heart of their victims with agonizing stings that are known only in the deep secrets of the soul. A dark and secret hour of retribution is at hand for Charles; the heavy but merciful hand of God will touch her, although she will still follow the mad career of her hypocrisy and the wild dreams of her ambition.

Alvira, still in her disguise of Charles, endeavored to forget the crimes she committed in the dissipation in which she indulged. Whilst wealth and friends were around she feigned a gay heart and flattered herself she was not so bad. She involuntarily blushed at rude remarks made by gentlemen amongst whom she passed as a companion, and in the unsullied innocence of her sister she found a guardian for herself. They invariably shunned low society, and thus they won the esteem of all; they passed as young men of virtue as well as of beauty and of grace. The immorality that dishonored the manhood around them, the indecency of the conversations they heard, and the open and blasphemous impiety that often thrilled their dove-like hearts, made them form a pleasing contrast with themselves and the corrupted society they had now known to the core; yet, "Say not I have sinned, and what evil hath befallen me." Who can flee from the eye of God? There's a sting in the conviction of guilt that will follow its victim through the ball-room, the mountain cave, or the cloister, to the very side of the bed of death.

It was when Charles and Henry found their money nearly gone, and the prospect of poverty before them, they felt in all its painful anticipations the prospect of a gloomy and unknown future. There is no pang, perhaps, in nature so keen as that which pierces the rich and ambitious when certain poverty stares them in the face; perhaps 'tis shame, perhaps 'tis pride, perhaps 'tis the despair that arises from the shock of blasted hopes—or all together—that weigh on the sinking heart, and make each vital throb like the last heavy thud of death. Then suicide has a charm and self-destruction a temptation. Many a turbulent wave has closed the career of the beggared spendthrift and the thwarted man of ambition.

Charles commenced now to suffer in anticipation all the pangs of coming shame, poverty, and humiliation. With remorse returned the virtuous impressions of childhood, instilled into her tender mind by her penitent mother. She longed to return to the circle nature had destined for her, but which seemed more difficult now than to commence a new disguise. Although she yielded in all virtuous impulses to that "procrastination which is the thief of time," yet in her after-career there was a wonderful combination of events, extraordinary and interesting, which prove a loving and forgiving Providence hearing the prayer of a penitent mother. But we must raise the curtain and proceed with the drama of sacred romance whose first acts have given so much interest and sympathy.

CHAPTER XVIII.

IN UNIFORM.

It was a bright morning in November, in the year 1684. The people of Milan were all flocking to the cathedral. It was the feast of the great St. Charles. The magnificent Duomo which now covers the shrine of this great saint was not in existence then; nevertheless, the devotion of the people towards their apostle and patron was deep and sincere. Perhaps in no city in Italy is there greater pomp thrown around the patron's festival than at Milan. From morning to night thousands gather around that venerated shrine. The prince with his liveried servants, and the poor peasant with the snow-white handkerchief tied on her head, kneel there side by side. From the first anniversary of the great saint's death to the present day the musical services of the cathedral have been rendered by the greatest talent in Italy, Professionals and amateurs flocked from every side to do honor to the man who did so much honor to the city of Milan. Nowadays, since science has shortened distance, it is one of the autumnal amusements of the wealthy Englishman to be present at the Feast of St. Charles at Milan. The gorgeous Duomo, hewn, as it were, out of Carrara marble, covered with five thousand statues and pinnacles, illumined with hundreds of thousands of lights swinging in the lofty aisles in chandeliers of sparkling crystal; the majestic organs, accompanied in musical harmony by hundreds of the best of human voices, rolling in soul-stirring majesty over the heads of tens of thousands of the kneeling children of the saint—all leave an impression never to be forgotten. Although in modern days the city of Milan has nurtured in her bosom some of the firebrands of Italian revolution, yet the city honored with the names and relics of Ambrose,

Augustine, and Charles has yet thousands of pious and holy souls, who still gather with filial devotion around the tombs of the sainted dead.

On the morning of the festival of St. Charles our heroine awoke with a heavy heart. She knew the city was astir and repairing to the cathedral. How strange she should have chosen the name of Charles! How great, how holy everything connected with that name! Could the man of God who made it so venerable to his people meet the wretch who had assumed it to dishonor it? Could even the pious people who flocked to the cathedral know there was amongst them a Charles whose hands were stained with parricidal guilt? Like the wicked man who fleeth when no man pursueth, Charles trembled lest the indignation of the people, of the saint, and of God should crush her in punishment of her sins.

With thoughts like these she entered the cathedral. Henry was by her side. The Pontifical High Mass had commenced, and the organ rolled its majestic tones through the aisles of the old church. Immense crowds had already gathered around the tomb, and Charles and Henry repaired to a quiet and obscure portion of the building, where they could observe without being observed.

Some years had now passed since Charles had breathed a prayer. There was something in everything around her that softened her heart; she buried her face in her hands and wept. An eloquent panegyric was preached by a Dominican Father. The peroration was an appeal to the assembled thousands to kneel and implore the blessing of the saint on the city and on themselves. Few sent a more fervent appeal than the poor, sinful girls who shunned the gaze of the crowd. The prayer of Charles was heard, and God, who works wonders in the least of his works, brought about the conversion of this child of predestination in a manner as strange as it is interesting.

The crowd have left the cathedral.

The lights are extinguished. The service is over. Charles and Henry were amongst the last to leave. On coming into the great square before the church they were surprised to see large groups of men in deep conversation. Their excited and animated manner showed at once something strange had happened. Men of strange dress appeared also in the crowd. Charles enquired what was the matter, and was informed that word had just come that Charles II. of Spain had declared war with Naples, and, as the state of Milan was subsidiary to the kingdom of the latter, he had sent officers to cause an enrolment of troops. Large inducements were offered to all who would join, and numbers of the youth of the city had already given in their names.

Charles scarcely hesitated in coming to a conclusion. The reduced state of their circumstances, the perfection of her disguise, and the still unconquered ambition of her heart made the circumstance a change of golden hope in the sinking prospects of her career. One thought alone deterred her. Could the delicate frame and soul of her little sister bear the hardships of a soldier's life? She breathed her thoughts to Henry. The latter cried and trembled. The one and only scene of blood she had witnessed still haunted her soul with horror—'twas in the ravine near Chamounix. But Charles still urged on the necessity of some desperate movement, and persuaded her, if they succeeded in joining this new service as officers, their position would be much the same as that they had passed through during the last two years. Poor Henry had but one tie to live for in the world; she preferred death to separation from her sister, and in the bravery of sisterly affection she told Charles she would swim by her side in the river of blood she might cause to flow.

The next morning found them enrolled as officers in the army of the King of Naples.

CHAPTER XIX.

REMORSE.

They call'd her cold and proud,
  Because her lip and brow
Amid the mirthful crowd
  No kindred mirth avowed;
Alas! nor look nor language e'er reveal
How much the sad can love, the lonely feel.

The peopled earth appears
  A dreary desert wide;
Her gloominess and tears
  The stern and gay deride.
O God! life's heartless mockeries who can bear
When grief is dumb and deep thought brings despair?

DURING the terrible storm that passed over the Church at the commencement of the third century, we have a thrilling incident which shows the terror and remorse of the pagan emperors when they returned to their golden house after witnessing the execution of their martyred victims.

Diocletian, being enraged with Adrian,

the governor of Antinoë—who, from being an ardent persecutor of the Church, had become a fervent follower of Christ—caused him to be dragged to Nicomedia, where, seized with implacable rage at the sight of the constancy of the martyr, who had once been his friend and confidant, he ordered him to be thrown, chained hand and foot, at the decline of day, into a deep pit, which was filled with earth and stones before the emperor's eyes. When the last cry of the victim had been stifled under the accumulated earth, the emperor stamped on it with his feet and cried out in a tone of defiance: " Now, Adrian, if thy Christ loves thee, let him show it."

He then quitted the field of punishment, but felt himself so overpowered by such an extraordinary feeling that he knew not whether it was the termination of his passion or the commencement of his remorse. His Thessalian courtiers bore him rapidly away from the accursed spot. Night fell; Diocletian, agitated and restless, prepared to retire to rest, for his head was burning.

He entered his chamber, which was hung around with purple, but the walls of which now seemed to distil blood. He advanced a few steps, when, lo! a corpse appeared to rise slowly on his golden couch; his bed was occupied by a spectre, and near the costly lamp, which shed a pale light round the chamber, the chains of the martyr seemed to descend from the ceiling. Diocletian uttered a cry that might have penetrated the grave. His guards ran in, but instantly grew pale, drew back, and, pointing to the object which caused an icy sweat to cover the imperial brow, they said with horror to each other: "IT IS THE CHRISTIAN."

Thus a guilty conscience summons imaginary terrors around it. Cain fled when no one pursued. Nero heard invisible trumpets ringing his death-knell around the tomb of his mother. How often has the mountain bandit, whose hand trembled not at murder, shuddered with fear, as he hastened through the forest, at the sound of a branch waving in the wind, or felt his hair stand erect with terror on beholding a distant bush fantastically enlightened by the moon! Conscience has made cowards of the most sanguinary freebooters and the most shameless oppressors. The dreadful " worm that dieth not," and banishes every cheerful thought from the guilty soul, is not inaptly compared to the wretch we read of in the annals of Eastern crime, condemned to carry about with him the dead and decomposing body of his murdered victim.

It is not to be expected that Charles escaped the agonies of a guilty conscience. From the moment she left the church in Milan the usual and dreadful struggle between shame and grace, humility and pride, commenced in her heart. Although now and then forgotten in the excitement of the extraordinary disguise she had assumed, nevertheless the feeling of remorse dampened every pleasure, and added to the disguise of her person another disguise of false joy to her countenance. This reaction caused an important feature in the life of Alvira during her stay in the beautiful town of Messina, whither we must ask our reader to follow our heroines to commence in their military career the most interesting part of this historical romance.

The Milanese recruits were busily engaged in going through military instruction, when orders were received that the division should sail immediately for Messina. There are few acquainted with the military life who do not know how disagreeable are orders to move. The bustle, the packing, the breaking up of associations, and the inevitable want of comfort in the military march try the courage of the brave man more than the din of battle, and robs the military career of much of its boasted enthusiasm. The stalwart son of Mars, who forgets there are such things as danger and fatigue in the exciting hour of battle, will grumble his discontent at the inconveniences of the hour of peace. We will leave it to the imagination of the reader to conceive the feelings, the regrets and misgivings, of our young heroines as their little vessel set sail from the town of Spezzia for the fortress of Messina. Although their biographers say nothing of their voyage, we cannot but imagine it was an unpleasant one. Although the blue headlands of the Italian coast, and the snow-capped Apennines in the distance, supplied the place of the compass, and their calls at the different ports deprived their journey of the painful monotony of a long sea-voyage, yet the associations, the cloud that hung over their thoughts, embittered every source of pleasure.

Arrived at Messina, Charles and Henry were quartered in the old fortress. It was an antiquated, quadrangular edifice, perched high up on the side of the hill, looking down on beautiful white houses built one over the other, and descending in terraces to the sea. Its old walls were dilapidated and disco'ored by the touch of time, and threatened every minute, as it afterwards did in the earthquake of 1769, to commence the awful avalanche of destruction that swept this fair city into the sea.

The first glimpse of their barracks did not rouse in Henry any ejaculations of gladness. The old Castello, as the people called it, ill-agreed with the noble edifices she was wont to call castles in her earlier days—no lofty battlements crested with clouds; no drawbridges swung on ponderous chains; no mysterious keeps haunted with traditionary horrors; no myriads of archers in gold and blue to rend the heavens with a mighty shout of welcome. Alvira's dream of military glory was a veritable castle in the air in the presence of the ruinous, ill kept, and dilapidated fortress they had come to reinforce.

Everything around seemed to increase the gloom that hung over Charles's heart. The ill-clad and poverty-stricken people, squatting in idleness and dirt in the streets; the miserable shops; the *dolce far niente* so conspicuously characteristic of Italian towns, were contrasted with the beautiful and busy capitals Charles and Henry had come from. But nowhere was this contrast so keen as in their domestic arrangements. The bleak apartments, the camp-bed, the iron washstand, and the rough cuisine contrasted sadly with the magnificence of their father's splendid mansion in Paris. No wonder our young heroines wept when alone over the memories of the past.

Charles and Henry kept together; they avoided all society; they loved to ramble along the beautiful beach that ran for some miles on the north side of the town, and there, in floods of tears, seek relief for their broken hearts. Oh! how memory will on these occasions wake up the happy past lost and gone, and the wicked past yet to be atoned for. What heart weighted with the agony of remorse will not feel the sting of guilt more keen in the remembrance of the blissful days of innocence and childhood? Many a blue wave has wrapt in its icy shroud the child of misfortune who was unable to bear the shame and reproof of her own conscience. It was in the recollection of virtuous childhood that Charles and Henry felt their greatest sorrows. Every tender admonition of their dying mother; the instruction of the aged abbé who prepared them for their first confession and communion; and the piety and noble example of their little brother, Louis Marie, who had fled in his childhood from the world they now hated, were subjects often brought up in their lonely rambles.

At night Charles would often awake with frightful dreams. The cold, blood-stained face of her murdered father would come in awful proximity to her. Her screams would bring her fellow-officers to her assistance, but they knew not the cause of her terror. The young officers had the sympathy of the whole garrison; even the people who saw them return from their evening walk remarked them to be lonely and sad, and their eyes often red from crying.

Three long and miserable months were thus passed by our heroines at Messina. They were now as skilful in their military exercises as they were in their disguise. But wearied of the military life, and longing to return to the society of their sex, they had determined to leave, to declare who they were, and endeavor, by some means, to get back to France. Whilst deliberating on this movement an incident occurred which changed their plans and cast them again into an extraordinary circle of vicissitudes.

CHAPTER XX.

NAPLES.

Whilst Charles and Henry were one evening walking along the beautiful beach they saw a ship nearing the land. A strong breeze was blowing at the time, and whilst they paused to admire the noble bark, all sails set, ploughing the crested billows, and floating over them like an enormous sea-gull, she came nearer and nearer to the young officers. Another minute the sails were lowered and anchor was cast. A small boat was despatched from the ship, and made for the beach just where Charles and Henry were standing. They formed a thousand conjectures of the meaning of this movement. When the boat came near the land, a tall young man, dressed in the uniform of the Neapolitan service, leaped on shore and advanced towards the young officers.

A few words of recognition passed. He was a lieutenant in the Neapolitan army, sent with despatches for the commandant of the garrison of Messina to send two or three companies of the newly-enrolled troops to the capital.

On the way to the garrison he informed Charles and Henry that the war was nearly at an end, but there was a great deal of disturbance and sedition in the city of Naples, and that the garrison there had to be doubled. The object in anchoring the ship on the coast was for fear the garrison of Messina might have been surprised and taken by the Carlists. Having assured himself all was safe, he entered the citadel with the young officers, and was presented to the captain, to whom he handed his despatches from headquarters.

The next evening found Henry and Charles, with two hundred men, on board the ship that had anchored on the coast the day before. The excitement and bustle of departure had silenced for a while all feelings of remorse, and the old passions that reigned in the soul of Charles rose again from their dormant state. Her eye flashed with life and her lips quivered with joy; there was still within her grasp the chance of fame. Ambition fanned the dying embers of decaying hope, and every pious resolve was thrown aside until the course of events would realize or blast her new dream of greatness.

A few days brought them in sight of the beautiful capital of the south of Italy. The modern aphorism, "See Naples and then die," was said in other words in old times, when the Cæsars and Senators of the empire enriched its beautiful shores with superb villas. There is not in Europe a bluer sky and, true in its reflection of the azure firmament, a bluer sea than around Naples. The coast undulates to the sea in verdant slopes, which in autumn have a rich golden hue from the yellow tinge of the vine-leaf. Its classic fame casts a halo around its charms; its history in the far past, its terrible mountain and periodical convulsions from the burning womb of the earth, render it an object of attraction to all classes.

Charles and Henry were quite alive to the impressions felt by tourists when, whirled along by the panting steam-horse through the luxuriant Campo Felice, they see for the first time the column of murky smoke that rises to the clouds over the terrible Vesuvius. The old mountain was then, as it is now, the terror and the attraction of tourists. The catastrophes it has caused, the cities it has swallowed up in molten ashes, the thunder of its roar when roused from its sleep, and the unhealthy, sulphurous vapors ever vomited from its cone, render it a veritable giant that the human race loves to see at a distance.

Our heroines were already acquainted with the "Light-house of the Mediterranean," and from afar the lofty and ever-blazing, active Etna; hence Vesuvius was not so attractive as a volcano as in the halo of classic lore that hung around it. At a distance the mountain seems to be harmless, the blue outline of the lofty cone terminating in a dense bank of smoke, like stormclouds gathering around the snowy peaks of the distant Apennines; but when the adventurous tourist wishes to approach nearer to its blazing crater, and toils up its torn and blackened sides, he will see in the immense chasms and rents traces of mighty convulsions. Deep rivers of molten lava that take twenty and thirty years to cool; the quantity of ashes and cinders that could change the whole face of a country and bury five cities in a few hours, must tell of the enormous furnace raging in the bowels of the earth, of which Vesuvius is but its chimney.

Strange, Charles longed to see Vesuvius when but a tender girl in Paris. She little thought the extraordinary course of human events would bring her, not only under the shadow of the terrible mountain itself, but send her through a most thrilling scene on its barren slopes. Let us hasten on to the course of events that rendered the extraordinary life of this girl so romantic.

CHAPTER XXI.

ENGAGEMENT WITH BRIGANDS.

ARRIVED in Naples, our heroines were quartered in the Molo. This is an old fortress still used as a barrack in Naples. Its massive, quadrangular walls were erected in the middle ages, and have withstood many a desperate siege in the civil wars of Italy.

The detachment from the Messina garrison found the city in a state of disturbance and confusion. Armed troops paraded the streets, houses were burning on every side, and bands of revolutionists were running frantically to and fro through the streets, yelling in the most unearthly tones their whoops of political antagonism to the Government; yet it was evident the Government had the upper hand, and the mob was gradually dispersing; they fled from the city, and order was restored. In the meantime word was received in Naples that a large body of these ruffians had settled themselves on the sides of Vesuvius, and supported themselves by the wholesale plunder and pillage of the farms and villages on the slopes of the hill. An order was immediately given that two hundred men should march to the mountain to destroy this band of brigands. The company selected was that belonging to Charles and Henry.

The next day found our young heroines on the road to the field of battle. We can fancy the position and thoughts of those tender, delicate girls, marching side by side with the rough, bearded soldiers of Italy—the one rejoicing in the wild dream of her foolish ambition; the other trembling in her timid heart, and dragged into scenes she loathed by the irresistible chain of affection which bound her to her sister.

No wonder the tender frame of girlhood yielded to the severities of the march—for amongst those who were first to fail was the amiable Henry; yet there were amongst the troops men whose constitutions were shattered by the excesses of their youth, and Henry became less remarkable as a young officer when stalwart men who had felt ere then the fatigues of war were falling at her side. Charles hired a horse in one of the villages they passed through, and thus arrived fresh and strong at the place of encampment, a few miles from the stronghold of the brigands. Henry came up in the afternoon, accompanied by about thirty men who, like herself, failed under the fatigues of the march.

Rest under the circumstances was impossible. The brigands were all around, and no one could tell the moment of attack. Some men were sent on as scouts to explore the hillside; they never returned. This was sufficient indication of an ambuscade, and the captain bravely determined to march his whole force at once into their hiding-place, knowing, when they were once surprised, they had no shelter afterwards.

Those who have been to Mount Vesuvius, and who have had the hardihood to seek the exquisite Lacryma produced on the southwestern slopes of the hill, will remember a peculiar ravine running for nearly a mile from the sandy part of the cone, and covered with a stunted green bush of fern-like leaves. It opens wider at one part nearly facing Sorento, and is more covered with small trees and evergreens. It is the nearest green spot to the calcined cone. It assumes a gentle declivity towards the sea, and is then lost in the beautiful vineyards and gardens that cover the slopes of the mountain down to the houses of Torre del Greco. The view from this spot is magnificent. On the left is the beautiful town of Sorento, with houses as white as snow, running in detached villas along the sea-shore up to the smoky and roofless walls of Pompeii, whose unsightly ruins lend contrast to the scene around. The azure bay seems to borrow more of the blue of heaven as it stretches far away to the horizon; the little steamers and innumerable yachts that ply between the islands give the scene animation and variety. Around to the right we have the classic hills of Baia, the Campo Santo in its fantastic architecture, and then the green and leafy plains of the Campo Felice; beneath, the great city with its four hundred thousand souls, its red tiles and irregular masses of brick-work, contrasting with the gilded domes of the superb churches; and above, the terrible cone, vomiting forth its sulphurous smoke and darkening the sky with clouds of its own creation.

The view that can be had from this place, and the interesting history of every inch of the country around, render it one of the most romantic spots in the world. But, alas! it is now, as it was two hundred years ago, the home and retreat of those desperate Italian robbers known as brigands. Woe betide the incautious traveller whom curiosity leads through the vineyards of that lonely scene! The deeds of its outlawed and daring inhabitants would fill volumes. It was here, too, as far as we can learn, our heroines found their field of battle.

The troops had scarcely entered this ravine when a sharp, shrill whistle rang from one side of the mountain to the other. Immediately human voices were heard on all sides, repeating in every pitch of tone, from bass to soprano, the word " Rione." For several minutes the mountain echoed with the weird sound of the brigand war-cry; the troops were ordered to stand in readiness, and timid hearts like Henry's quailed at the awful moment.

The earth rumbled under their feet, and dark, bluish columns of smoke curled into the air from the terrible cone; the sun was setting over the beautiful Bay of Naples in the color of blood, and the air was impregnated with the fumes of sulphur. The wildness of the spot, and nature's terrors convulsing the elements around, made, indeed, the moment before battle a dreadful moment for the delicate children of the French banker.

A few minutes, and the battle was at its height. A long and dreadful contest ensued. The numbers were about equal on both sides. Fortunately, the brigands had not time to muster all at once, and the royalist troops met them in small but desperate bands. No sooner was one defeated than another and another poured down from the sides of the mountain and disputed every inch of the way. The brigands fought bravely, but were outnumbered, and towards midnight the bloodshed ceased. All sounds had died away save the groans of the wounded and dying, and now and then a solitary whoop of a brigand chief from the distant hills, calling together the few straggling and scattered bands of rebels.

The moment the heat of the combat was over the first thought that struck Charles was to look for Henry. They were separated in the confusion of the fight. She ran through the men, but could not find her. Here and there she could discern in the pale light of a clouded moon some knots of soldiers binding up their wounds and recounting their escapes and their triumphs. She hurriedly ran through them, enquiring for her brother-officer, but none knew anything of her. She scanned every feature, she called her in every group, but in vain—no Henry was there. The awful thought struck her—and her heart nearly broke under its pang—perhaps she is killed! She flew across the bloody path they had passed; her mournful and shrill cry of "Enrico!" rolled over the bodies of the slain, and was echoed again and again with plaintive intensity from the surrounding hills. Sometimes she even fancied the dying echo of her own shrill cry was the feeble answer of her wounded sister; and when she would pause to listen again, the valley around was wrapt in the stillness of death. At length she came to the spot where the battle first commenced, and there, with a shriek that was heard in the distant encampment, she found among the first victims of that bloody night the lifeless corpse of her sister.

CHAPTER XXII.

THE MORNING AFTER THE BATTLE.

THE morning sun rose dimly in a bank of clouds. It found Charles still clinging to the remains of poor Aloysia, and bathing with kisses and tears the stiffened features of her beloved sister. With a silken kerchief she had bandaged the fatal gash on her neck, believing she might be only in a swoon and might recover. Hope, which is the last comfort to abandon man in his most desperate condition, scarcely retarded for Charles the awful reality of her bereavement.

The pale moon that has rolled over so many generations, and lent its dim, silvery light to so many thrilling vicissitudes, never looked down on a sadder scene. Death has no pang equal to the blow it gives true affection. No language could describe what the heart feels on occasions like this. There sat the delicate French girl, alone in the dark night, on the side of Vesuvius, in the midst of the bleeding victims of the bloody fight, and clasping to her heart the cold, lifeless body of her ill-fated sister.

Her sudden and awful end, swept, perhaps, into eternity without a moment's notice, to be buried in the ashes of the volcano, amidst the dishonored remains of outlaws and murderers—does not the thought strike us that this sad fate was more the due of Alvira than the innocent and harmless Aloysia?

Alvira felt it, and her repentant heart was almost broke.

"O Aloysia!" hear her moan over the angelic form, " you innocent and I guilty; you slain, judged, and I free to heap greater ingratitude on the Being who has saved me. Aloysia, forgive! Thou wert dragged unwillingly to these desperate scenes of bloodshed by my infatuation. O God! strike me. I am the wretch; let this angel live to honor thee in the angelic simplicity of her innocence!"

Never was a fairer flower blasted by the lightning of Heaven. Neither Charles nor Henry knew what was before them in their march to Vesuvius. To surround and capture a few runaways was perhaps the most they expected; and Henry, in the confiding affection of her heart, clung to Charles, determined to bear fatigue and hardship rather than be separated from her.

It must be a painful picture that fancy will paint of the last hour of this lovely child. The anguish of her heart must have been keener than the deep wound that sent the life-streams to mingle with the lava of the mountain: no one to minister a drop of water to her parched lips; no friendly voice to console her; the moans and imprecations of the wounded brigands grating on her ears; the thought that her sister, too, was perhaps lying in pain, and sinking from her wounds; and, above all—

that which, perhaps, sent the last blush to her cheek—the fear of the discovery of her sex, and the rough gaze of a brutal soldiery. But Heaven's sympathizing spirits were gathered around this child of misfortune, and doubtless with her last sigh she breathed her pure soul into their hands, and the last wish was answered—for she was good and innocent before God.

When the sun had fully risen, Charles was approached by a sergeant of the troops, who announced to her that the captain had died during the night from his wounds, and, as she was the senior officer, they waited her orders. Dissembling her grief, Charles rose to her feet and gave directions that the bodies of the captain and her brother should be buried in their clothes and wrapped in the flag of the country. The hardy veterans raised the delicate frame of Henry, and carried it on a rude bier to the hut where the remains of the captain were prepared for interment. Silent and solemn was the funeral cortége. No drum, not a funeral note, was heard.

Every eye was wet, and the breast of Charles was not the only one that heaved the farewell sigh over the young and beautiful officer.

Charles stood by to see the last of her sister. The dark, black sand was poured down on her lovely face, and silently and quickly her mountain grave was filled by the blood-stained hands of her companions in arms.

CHAPTER XXIII.

RETURN—A TRIUMPH.

CHARLES has dreamt a golden dream. Ambition's cup is full, but its draught is bitter. On the march to Naples, in triumph, commanding the royal troops, who had completely beaten the brigands, were glories Charles never thought she was one day to obtain. With her return to the city the war was ended, and the people were rejoicing in the restoration of peace. The young captain who had returned so victorious from Vesuvius was the lion of the day. The city gave her an ovation far beyond her most sanguine hopes. Illuminations were instituted in her honor, her name was shouted in the streets, and the nobles and great ones of the state gathered around her as if the safety of the kingdom had depended on her own personal efforts. For some time crowds of lazzaroli gathered around the entrance of the Molo to see the young and beautiful captain who had achieved such wonders; and we can fancy how sweetly would ring on the ears of our ambitious heroine the shout of the enthusiastic crowd sending far and wide the "Erira Carlo Pimontel!" The King confirmed her position of captain, and sent her the iron and golden crosses of honor, only given to the bravest of the brave in those days of strife and warfare.

But vanity of vanities, and all is vanity! Let us raise the veil of deception that shrouds the emptiness of human joy. Alvira has now gratified her heart's desires in everything she could have under the sun. She had beauty, wealth, and fame, but she was like the pretty moth that hovers around the flame of the candle, and finds its ruin in the touch of the splendor it loves. Poor Alvira was another child of Solomon that sighed over the emptiness of human joy; for bitter disappointment is the sad tale ever told in the realization of misguided hope. Often, at midnight, when the unknown captain would return from the theatre or some festive entertainment given in her honor, she would sit at her table, wearied and disgusted, and weep bitterly. The unnatural restraint necessary to preserve her disguise, the separation from all the comforts and sympathies common to her sex, and the painful reminiscences of the past wrung tears of misery from her aching heart. The dreams of Messina haunted her still, but increased in anguish and terror, as her thoughts could now fly from the lonely cave on the Alps to the battle-field on the side of Vesuvius. Again the pangs of remorse poisoned every joy; again the angry countenance and clenched hand of her murdered father would bend over her restless couch; and again the scream of terror in the dark, silent midnight would summon her friends around her. Deep and fervent the prayer that was poured forth from that sad and breaking heart that some providential circumstance would enable her to make the change she had now long premeditated. That change is at hand. Her mother's prayer is still pleading for her before the throne of God; he who cast an eye of mercy on the erring Magdalen had already written the name of Alvira in the book of life, and destined her to be one of the noblest models of repentance that adorn the latter history of the Church. Let us come to the sequel of this extraordinary history; but first we must introduce our readers to a new character—a great and holy man, destined by Providence to save Alvira, and give the most interesting and most remarkable chapter in this romance of real life.

CHAPTER XXIV.

ALVIRA'S CONFESSION.

> Tremble, thou wretch,
> Thou hast within thee undivulged crimes,
> Unwhipped of justice : hide thee, thou bloody hand ;
> Thou perjured, and thou simular man of virtue,
> Thou art incestuous : caitiff, to pieces shake,
> That under covert and convenient seeming
> Hast practised on man's life : close pent-up guilts,
> Rive your concealing continents, and cry
> These dreadful summoners grace.
> —LEAR.

IT was a beautiful morning in the Lent of 1678. The sun had risen over the Apennines, and flung its magnificence over the Bay of Naples. The smoke of Vesuvius cast its shadow like a monstrous pine over the vineyards and villas that adorned the mountain-side to the sea-shore. The morning was such as Byron gazed on in fancy through the sorrowful eyes of the eloquent heroine of one of his tragedies:

"So bright, so rolling back the clouds into
 Vapors more lovely than the unclouded sky,
 With golden pinnacles and snowy mountains,
 And billows purpler than the ocean's, making
 In heaven a glorious mockery of the earth,
 So like we almost deem it permanent,
 So fleeting we can scarcely call it aught
 Beyond a vision, 'tis so transiently
 Scattered along the eternal vault!"

Whilst the eighth hour was chiming from the tower of the old Gesù there issued from the monastery attached to the church a priest accompanied by an acolyte bearing a large, plain cross and ringing a small bell. They moved in the direction of the mole or old fortress of the city. Soon a crowd followed—some bare-headed; others, especially the females, told their beads in silence.

The traveller in Italy is aware of the pious custom practised by some of the religious communities of preaching in the open air to the people during the season of Lent. Extraordinary things are related of these harangues. The lives of the sainted missionaries ring with tales of the marvellous and miraculous powers given to God's servants when, in moments of fire and zeal, they went from their cloisters like beings of another world to awaken sinners to a sense of future terrors. At one time we read of the saint's voice carried miraculously to a distance of several miles; the peasant working in the fields would hear the sweet sounds without seeing the speaker. At another the funeral procession was arrested and the dead called from the bier to testify to the truth of their teaching. Curing the cripple and restoring health to the sick were of ordinary occurrence. Our blessed Lord told the messengers who came to enquire about him to report his miracles as a proof of his divinity: the blind see, the lame walk, the sick are restored to health; but greater than all his reversions of the natural laws were the humility and the mysterious ar-arrangement of his providence which he prophetically announced when he told his disciples that those who should come after him would perform greater miracles than he. There are few of the Thaumaturgi more celebrated than the humble father who has just issued from the Gesù to thunder forth with superhuman eloquence the truths of God and religion.

No sooner had the people heard the little bell of the attendant and seen the venerable priest leave the college than they gathered from various quarters, and seemed to vie with each other in getting nearest to him.

He was a tall, thin man, his hair gray, shading a majestic forehead, and but slightly wrinkled with the summers of over sixty years; his eyes were partly closed, but when preaching they glowed with animation, and were brightened by the tears that dimmed them; his long, wiry fingers were interlocked and raised towards his breast in the attitude of deep contemplation. The rough soutane and leather belt, the beads and missionary cross partly hid in his breast, declared him to be a follower of St. Ignatius. In the hallowed austerity of his whole appearance, in the sweetness blended with religious gravity, and in the respect and love manifested in the ever-increasing crowd, one easily learned he was more than an ordinary man. The people of Naples knew him by the endearing name of Brother Francis; history has since written his name in letters of gold on the altars of the Catholic Church as St. Francis of Jerome.

It must have been a treat to the people who heard such saints as Francis of Jerome preach. Natural eloquence is a rare and powerful gift; when guided by education and study, the talent exercises a marvellous influence on man; but add to these two a zeal and fervor of spirit such as burned in the mortified spirit of the man of God, and we have a power that is nothing short of supernatural and irresistible.

From a heart all aglow with divine love he soon enkindled in his hearers that fire his divine Master came to kindle on earth. His sermons were miracles. So great was the crowd around him at times that it would be impossible for any human voice to reach his furthest hearers. Yet every word of the great preacher went with silvery tone and moving power, as if wafted on angel breathings, to the ears of sinners whom chance or grace had brought to join the immense crowd that surrounded his rude platform. Each sermon brought hundreds to repentance. Eyes that were long dry melted into tears, and hearts that were strangers to every sweet and holy influence throbbed with emotion. Efforts to check the pent-up feelings were expressed by louder and convulsive sobs; some knelt and prayed, others beat their breasts in the agony of contrition. The immense concourse of people, simple and religious minded, at all times impressionable, were, under the appeals of Francis, moved as in times of public calamity, and the whole crowd swayed to and fro as the deep moved by the storm—now trembling in terror, now ashamed of sin and ingratitude, and again encouraged with hope, whose cheerful beams the orator would cause to dart through the dark clouds he himself had gathered over their mental vision.

On one occasion a courtesan ridiculed from her bed-room window the words of the saint. She fell dead immediately. When he heard of the awful judgment passed on this hapless woman, he ordered her body to be brought to him. Then, amidst a deathlike silence, he cried out in a voice of thunder that penetrated the regions of the damned: "Catherine, where art thou now?"

The soul answered with a shriek that sent a thrill through the assembled thousands: "In hell!"

Although in scenes of terror like these Francis thundered forth the awful destinies of the judged, yet the mercy of God towards the sinner was his favorite theme. He looked on himself as called in a special manner to seek out the lost sheep, to soften down the roughness found on the path of repentance, to aid in the struggles willing souls find in their efforts at reformation. Francis knew, as all masters of the spiritual life have learned, there is more power in the eloquence of forgiving love than in the terrors of retribution; hence, with tears and burning sentiments of sympathy for the erring children of men, he led his hearers as it were by the hand to the Father of the prodigal—to that Jesus who forgave and loved the penitent Magdalen.

Francis has now ascended his platform. The crowd are swelling around. He raises the sign of redemption over their heads; in a few majestic sentences he commences his subject; the fire is kindling in his eye, and the thunder is deepening in his splendid voice. The listeners are wrapt in breathless attention.

On the outskirts of the crowd there is a young officer, slender, graceful, tidy to a fault. It is Alvira.

She was passing down the Toledo, and had already heard the saint before she had seen him. She had heard of the great preacher, but was afraid to meet him. Grace had followed her in all her wanderings, and the prayers of her mother were still heard at the throne of God. The crowd is so great Alvira cannot pass to the Molo, where she was quartered with her regiment. She must listen.

Strange, consoling ways of divine grace! It was thee, O Lord! who drew thy servant from his convent on that auspicious morning; thou did'st gather the crowd around him, and inspire him with the words and theme of his moving discourse! It was thy mercy, smiling with compassion on a noble but erring soul, which brought her to listen to those words that would bring thy grace to her heart!

Like one whose eye has caught a brilliant meteor flying through the heavens, and remains gazing on it until it has disappeared, Alvira could not remove her eyes from Francis. When she saw his saintly figure standing on the rude platform, holding in his outstretched hand the saving sign of redemption, she was seized with an unaccountable feeling of awe. Although every word of the sermon was heard and weighed, it seemed as if the pent-up memories of her soul took precedence of her thoughts, and rushed on her with overwhelming force, like the winds let loose by the storm-god of old. Everything strange or sad in her past career lent its quota of color to the dark picture remorse, with cruel and masterly hand, delineated before her troubled spirit. The struggle, the agony she had learned to brave in the Duomo at Milan and the fortress of Messina, rose again with hydra fangs from the tomb of oblivion in which recent excitements had buried it. None but her guardian angel knew her soul was once more the battle-field of contending feelings. At length a crimson blush passed over her marble features; a crystal tear-drop dimmed her eye; another sprang from the reservoirs of the heart and stole down the blushing cheek. Alvira wept.

Tears have a language of their own deep and powerful; they tell of the weakness of the human heart, not its triumphs; for passion has a throne that tears may wash in vain. It is easier to drive the mighty river from its long-loved bed than the soul from the normal state of its gratified tendencies.

"The heart," says St. Liguori, "where passion reigns, has become a crystal vase filled with earth no longer penetrated by the rays of the sun." The iron pedestal of passion's throne was not yet shivered in the heart of Alvira, nor were tears a sign that the sun of grace had pierced the crystal vase of the worldly heart. Great will be the grace that will draw Alvira from the zenith of a golden dream in which a triumphant ambition has placed her above her sex, and great amongst the heroes of the manly sex she feigned. Her conversion will be a miracle—a miracle of sweet violence, such as drew the Magdalens, the Augustines, and the Cortonas from the trammels of vice to the holy and happy path of repentance.

The sermon is over. The crowd is still between Alvira and the Molo; she must wait.

The people are gradually dispersing.

Some go to the church to follow up the holy inspirations given, to throw themselves at the feet of a confessor, to break the chains of sin; others hasten to their homes or daily avocations, wondering, pleased, and sanctified in good desires and resolutions that came gushing from their hearts.

Alvira is standing one side alone and wrapt in thought. Suddenly she looks up. Something catches her eye. She starts; a tremble passes from head to foot. She looks again; her worst terrors are realized. It is—Father Francis is coming towards her!

"But he can't be coming to me," she thought to herself. She looked around to see if there were any other object to bring the father in that direction; but there was no poor creature to ask his charity, no poor cripple to seek his sympathy; she was almost alone. She could have fled, but felt herself fixed to the ground, and with desperate efforts endeavored to conceal her excitement. He approaches nearer; with glistening eye she watches and hopes some fortuitous circumstance may call him aside. Their glance meets; she blushes and trembles. Father Francis is before her.

For a moment he gazed on the young captain with a kind, penetrating look; and a smile on his features seemed to express a friendly recognition. Calling her by her assumed name, he said to her, almost in a whisper: "Charles, go to confession; God wishes thee well."

Alvira was relieved. The kind, gentle manner of the father calmed the storm of conflicting fears. Rejecting the inward calls of grace, and hoping she was not discovered, she replied with some hesitation:

"But, father, I don't require to go to confession. I have not done anything wrong."

Her voice faltered, and the blush of conscious falsehood grew deeper and deeper on her glowing features.

Father Francis drew himself up with majesty; his eye beamed with the glow of inspiration, and in a solemn reproof he addressed the trembling girl:

"You have done nothing wrong, nothing to merit the judgments of a terrible God—you, who murdered your father in the snows of the Alps, robbed him of ill-gotten wealth, spent it in gaming, and dragged your innocent sister in the path of your own shameless adventure!"

"Father! father!" cried Alvira, bursting into convulsive sobs.

"Maria Alvira Cassier," continued the man of God in a milder tone "go and change those garments; cease this tale of guilty hypocrisy. But—"

Advancing towards her, he took her hand, and, resuming the paternal smile that relaxed his solemn features and banished her fears, said in a low tone: "But come with me to the Gesù."

Alvira obeyed. She was thunderstruck. The revelation of the great secrets of her life summoned up paralyzing fears; but, accustomed to brave the succumbing weakness of the feminine character, and en couraged by the paternal manner of the father, she did not faint, but buried her face in her hands and wept.

In silence she followed Father Francis. She skilfully concealed her emotions; the tears were brushed away as rapidly as they overflowed. In passing the squares that separated them from the church, Alvira had resolved to unbosom herself to the good father. Like the angel that led Peter from his prison, she knew this sainted man was destined to lead her from the prison of her hypocrisy. Where grace has not conquered, consequences are weighed, the future becomes too dark and unknown for the cowardly heart, and temporal evils assume the weight of eternal woes; the blinded self-love yields, and the moment of grace is abandoned. But Alvira's conversion was complete, and, without one doubt or fear for the future, she handed herself to the guidance of the venerable father, who had learned by inspiration from heaven the spiritual maladies of her soul.

The whole of that day was spent in the church. She crouched into an angle behind one of the large pillars. Like the dew that freshens and vivifies the vegetation that has been dried up by the parching sun, the exhilarating breathings of the divine Spirit spread over her soul that peace which surpasseth all understanding. In the fervor of her first real moments of prayer, the hours passed as seconds; unmindful of food, of the duties incumbent on her military profession, and of the busy world around, she was not roused from her reverie until the golden floods of the seting sunlight fell in tinted splendor through the stained-glass windows of the old Gothic church.

As the church bells were merrily chiming the Ave Maria, a gentle tap on her shoulder called her attention. It was Father Francis. He had watched her all the day with a secret joy; he knew the value of moments like these in maturing the resolutions of the converted soul, and, as he had not yet completed his arrangements, he was afraid his penitent might slip from him in the crowd and be exposed to temptations that might discourage her; the cold blast of the world might shake to the ground the fabric he had commenced to build. He bent his venerable countenance to her ear, whispered a word of consolation, and bade her not leave till he came for her.

The father moved silently and thoughtfully through the sombre aisles; now and then he would stop to converse with some child of grace, for he had many awaiting his spiritual aid. With smiles of holy joy, he imparted consolation to each, and sent them to their homes accompanied by those spirits that rejoice in the conversion of the sinner.

A few moments, and the lights are extinguished, the crowd is gone. The cough and suppressed sigh are no longer heard from the deep aisles, and the footsteps of the ever-changing crowd have ceased to clatter on the marble pavement. The solitary lamp in the sanctuary cast a fitful shadow through the silent and abandoned church, and was the only indication of the presence of Him who rules in the vast spheres of the heavens. Alvira felt happier in this lonely moment before the Most Holy Sacrament. The fruit of years of penance, and the conquest of turbulent, rebellious passions, have often been gained in moments of fervor before the altar. Like sand, changed to transparent crystal glass under the blow-pipe, the heart is melted and purified under the fire of love that darts in invisible streams from the loving Victim of the tabernacle.

The closing of the church door and the rattling of carriage wheels in the direction of the Chaja close an eventful day, recorded in golden letters in heaven's history of repentant humanity.

CHAPTER XXV.

HONOR SAVED.

A SERIES of surprises followed this memorable conversion. Alvira's absence from the garrison was the subject of serious comment. Rumor was busy, and disposed of the young captain by every imaginable violent death. One report seemed the most probable and gained ground. It was thought the partisans of the defeated party, remembering the victory of Vesuvius, and galled at the popularity of the young captain, had waylaid and murdered him. At the same time the mangled body of a young man was found washed into the river by the tide; it was mutilated and disfigured beyond recognition; the populace claimed it to be the body of their favorite, and loud and shrill rang the indignant cry for vengeance. The city was in commotion. The authorities were induced to believe the report, and large rewards were offered for the apprehension of the murderers. 'Tis but a spark that may set the wood on fire; and popular feeling, fired by a random rumor, now blazed in all the fury of a political conflagration.

In the midst of the commotion the commandant of the forces received a polite note requesting his presence at the residence of the Marchioness de Stefano. Puzzled at the strange summons, but polite to a fault, he appeared in *grand tenu* at the appointed hour in the salons of the Marchioness. A young lady was ushered into the apartment She was dressed in black, wore no jewelry, and seemed a little confused; a majestic mien set off some natural charms, but her features had an expression of care and sadness such as is read on the countenance of the loving fair one who has been widowed in her bloom. Her eyes were red, for many tears had dimmed them; her voice was weak, for shame had choked the utterances in their birth; her whole demeanor expressed deep anxiety and trouble.

The commandant was kind-hearted, but a stern ruler in those days of trouble; he had seen in the revolutions of many years the miseries and sorrows of life; though insensible to the horrors of the battle-field, he felt a deep, touching sympathy with its real victims who survive and suffer for years in silent woe, in affections that have been ruthlessly blasted by cruel war. The feeling of compassion towards the strange lady introduced to him were deeply enhanced by the remarks by which she opened the conversation.

"I sent for you, sir," commenced the lady in a subdued tone, "to speak to you about Captain Charles Pimontel."

The veteran soldier, believing she was his betrothed, that she was torn by cruel destiny from the object of her affections, endeavored to soothe her troubled spirit by the balm of kindness and consolation.

"Ah! madame," he replied in his blandest manner, "if report be true, a cruel fate has removed him for a while from thy embrace. Young, brave, and amiable, he was the darling of our troops, and fortune seemed to lead our gallant young captain to a brilliant career; but some foul assassin's hand has cut the flower ere it bloomed; destiny, as cruel as it has been mysterious, has darkened his sun ere yet it shone in the zenith of day!"

"Oh! sir, it may not yet be true that he has met such a sad fate," retorted the lady.

"Alas!" replied the commandant, "yesterday evening the youth's body was washed up on our beach; the wounds of twenty stilettos gaped on his mangled corpse, and the lampreys of our bay fed on his noble flesh as they would on the vile slaves cast to them by the monster Nero. These eyes have seen the horrid sight; though we could not recognize the brave youth, we wept as if our own son had fallen by cowardly hands."

The old commandant was somewhat excited; before the warm tear had welled from the fountains of sympathy, the young lady spoke in an animated and excited manner :

"But, sir, there is surely some mistake. It cannot be said Charles Pimontel was murdered; does it follow because the unrecognized body of some hapless victim of a street brawl has been washed on the beach that it must necessarily be the body of the captain? Do you not think his murderers would pay dearly for this attack on him? Have any witnesses come forward to swear to his assassination? I will not believe in his death until stronger proofs have been given; and I may be intruding on the precious time of our commandant, but I have sought this interview with you to warn you against the popular rumor that you have found the murdered remains of Charles Pimontel."

"Love, madame," rejoined the commandant sentimentally, "clings to forlorn hopes, and in its sea of trouble will grasp at straws. The whole city has proclaimed the murder of the captain; our military chapel is draped in gloom, and I have given orders that all the garrison be in attendance on the morrow at the obsequies."

The lady, who at first intended a strange surprise for the commanding officer, began to fear things were going too far, and that no time was to be lost in declaring the real fate of the captain. She arose quickly, and, approaching near to him, spoke with strong emphasis:

"I beseech you, sir, to stay these proceedings; I tell you on my word of honor the captain is not dead."

"Then you know something of him?" interrupted the commandant. "I command you, madame, in the name of the King, to tell me of his whereabouts. If he has, without sufficient cause, absented himself from military duty, by my sword the rash youth shall be punished. Besides playing the fool with the people, the inviolable sanctity of the military constitutions has been violated. Madame, your lover, perhaps, has forgotten himself over his cups. If secreted within these walls, produce him, that he may know, for thy sake, and in consideration of his first fault, the leniency of his sentence for violation of our military rule."

"Sir," replied the young woman, drawing herself up majestically, and fearlessly confronting the aged officer, whose inviolable fidelity to military honor made him warm in his indignation at the supposed delinquency of his subaltern—"sir, the secret of the captain's absence and his present abode is committed to me; but I shall not divulge the information you ask until you promise me that, having shown you reasonable cause for his seeming fault, you will not only acquit him of his supposed crime of dereliction of duty, but that his honor shall be preserved unstained before his fellow-officers and men."

The proposition seemed honorable to the commandant, and he immediately replied:

"I swear by my sword it shall be so."

"Then, sir, see before you the offender. I am Charles Pimontel!"

CHAPTER XXVI.

REPENTANCE.

On the road that led the traveller to the ancient village of Torre del Greco, and about a mile from the populous parts of the city, there stood a neat little cottage. In the front there was a flower garden, small but charmingly pretty; the doors and windows were surrounded with a woodbine creeper that gave an air of comfort to the little dwelling. The door was ever closed. Few were seen to pass in and out, and no noise ever betrayed the presence of its inmates.

Here for many years our young penitent Alvira passed a holy and solitary life. After the stirring scenes of the preceding chapters, Father Francis procured from the military authorities for his Magdalen, as he was wont to call her, the full pay of a captain as a retiring pension. This remarkable circumstance may be authenticated by reference to the military books still preserved in the archives of the Molo at Naples. Her rank and pension were confirmed by the king.

Under the able direction of the man of God, Alvira gave herself to full correspondence with the extraordinary graces offered by our blessed Lord. Her austerities and fervor increased until they reached the degrees of heroic sanctity. She knelt and wept for hours before her crucifix; she slept on hard boards and only allowed herself sufficient to meet the demand of nature. She lived on herbs, and the fast of Lent was so severe that Father Francis saw a miraculous preservation. Long before daylight she knelt on the steps of the Gesù waiting for the opening of the doors, and this austerity she never failed to practise in the midst of rain or cold, until her last illness chained her involuntarily to her couch, where her submission to the will of God was equally meritorious.

Several terrible scenes of judgment, sent by Almighty God on unrepentant sinners, had, in the very commencement of her conversion, a most salutary influence on the feeble struggles of Alvira. Her confidence in the Blessed Virgin was much enhanced by a severe act of St. Francis towards one of the members of the Congregation of the Most Holy Mother.

A young man of this congregation got suddenly rich, and, with wealth, self-conceit and pride entered his heart. He considered it necessary, to preserve his respectability, to separate himself from the humble society he hitherto frequented, and cease to be a member of the Congregation of the Madonna, composed of industrious and virtuous youths who labored honestly for their livelihood. St. Francis, on hearing of this slight on the congregation and insult to Mary, was fired with a holy indignation. He sought the young man, and rang in his ears the prophetic warnings which, in the case of this great saint, were never uttered in vain to the unheeding. Again and again St. Francis warned, but pride was still triumphant. One Sunday afternoon, after the usual meeting of the confraternity, the saint went to the altar of sodality; it was the altar of the Dolors. Seven daggers seemed to pierce the Virgin's heart. Ascending the altar, he cast a sorrowful glance on the weeping countenance of the Queen of Sorrows, and said: "Most Holy Virgin, this young man has been for you a most acute sword, piercing your heart; behold, I will relieve you of it." So saying, he took one of the poniards from the statue, and at the same time announced to the members that the proud young man was expelled from the congregation.

Let those who fancy that such reprobations have not a corresponding echo in the judgments of God tremble in reading the effects of this simple but terrible excommunication.

Like sand through the perforated vessel, the young man's wealth passed away; one month found him a cringing debtor, another found him a beggar, a third found him dying in a public institution, abandoned by God and man.

On another occasion Alvira was present when a terrible judgment of God upon a hardened sinner thrilled the whole city with awe. St. Francis was preaching in one of the streets during Lent. He happened to pause and address a crowd near the house of an impious, ill conducted woman, who came immediately to her window to laugh and mock at the man of God. Having gratified herself to the disgust of the crowd, she finally slammed to the window violently, uttering at the same time some filthy and unbecoming remark. St. Francis stood immovable for a moment; his eye was fixed on heaven; and then, in a voice heard half over the city, he cried out: "My God, how terrible are thy judgments! That unfortunate woman has dropped dead."

The groans and confusion of the inmates soon convinced the crowd of the awful fact, for the corpse of the hapless wretch was brought into the street, where it was exposed to the terrified people.

These and similar instances of the judgment of God witnessed by Alvira had a salutary effection her trembling soul. The fear of God, which is the beginning of wisdom, erected its watch-tower around the citadel of her heart; the virtues, once entered, were not permitted to flee, and soon won for this penitent soul the sweets of the illuminative degree of sanctity.

St. Francis, a master in the science of the saints, soon recognized the extraordinary graces destined for this chosen soul. Full of gratitude and love for God, he spared no effort to correspond with the sublime destiny entrusted to him; hence in the after-history of those two holy souls the marvels of virtue and sanctity intermingled, so that at times it would seem doubtful whether the miracles recorded were given to the exalted sanctity and zeal of the holy priest or to the weeping virgin penitent, so privileged and so loved in the forgiving mercy of God.

On one occasion a young mother lost her infant. Death had stricken the little flower ere it had blossomed. The mother was poor and unable to bury the child. With an unbounded confidence in the charity and zeal of St. Francis, the bright thought struck her: If she could only get this good man interested in her behalf, all would be accomplished. Accordingly, she made for the church of the Gesù by daylight. Only one individual was before her waiting for the church to be opened. It was Magdalen. Even from Magdalen she concealed the object of her early visit, and pressed closer to her heart the dead treasure she intended as a present for Father Francis. The church opened; she stole around the dark aisles, whence the daylight had not yet banished the shades of night, and noiselessly approached the confessional of the holy man. She placed the dead child on the seat, and hurried to some recess of the great church, where she could watch the happy issue of this ingenious mode of disposing of her child. The early morning hours wore away, and at length the wished-for moment came. The vestry door is opened. The tall, mortified form of St. Francis appeared at the foot of the altar. He prayed awhile, and rose to go to his confessional. But the young mother watched with her heart leaping to her mouth. He did not go to his tribunal; he moved majestically down the church, and came to Magdalen's corner where Alvira was wrapt in prayer. He whispered something to her; they prayed a moment, then Alvira flitted like a shadow through the dark aisles towards the confessional of Father Francis. She entered and took the infant child in her arms. The child was alive. The mother came rushing from her hiding-place to claim the infant, and when she received it into her embrace the man of God raised his index finger in the act of warning, and with a sweet, forgiving smile on his countenance, said to the young mother: "My child, don't put any more dead babies in my confessional."

Alvira had to undergo a severe trial in the absence of Father Francis. He was directed by his superiors to commence his missions in the country districts, and was virtually removed from Naples for some years. Before leaving, he fortified his chosen children with salutary admonitions, but for Alvira he had special words of encouragement and consolation. It pleased God to let him know in her behalf that, in return for her sincere repentance and deep devotion to the Blessed Virgin, before her death three extraordinary favors would be conferred on her, which would also be the warning of the setting sun of her career in life. Alvira treasured his words in her heart, and in deep humility wondered at the goodness of God.

CHAPTER XXVII.

THE PRIVILEGES OF HOLY SOULS.

An extraordinary miracle is said, in the life of St. Francis, to have taken place in the house where Alvira was present. St. Francis had an aged brother living in the city—a man of eminent sanctity, but suffering much from his infirmities. St. Francis prevailed on Alvira to attend him and nurse him in his illness. He could not have been trusted to more tender or willing hands.

Virtue and affection lent their powerful aids to render Alvira a charming nurse. But her labor of love was not very protracted, for it pleased God to cast the last and fatal fever on Cataldus, the invalid brother of the saint. At the time the malady was increasing and death imminent,

St. Francis was absent from the city on a mission at Recale, a place about sixteen miles from Naples. Cataldus prayed to be permitted to see his brother before death but the malady seemed to increase so rapidly there was very slight probability of his return in time.

Alvira had retired to an adjoining apartment to seek relief in prayer. She suddenly heard some strange sounds in the room of her patient. She flew towards the chamber, and there, to her astonishment, she beheld St. Francis embracing his brother.

"Go," said the saintly man to the invalid—"go with courage and confidence whither God thy father calls thee, and where the saints await thee. Remember God is a good master, and know that in a short time I will follow thee."

Then drawing Alvira aside, he whispered to her: "My child, know that Cataldus is going with rapid strides to eternity. You must still assist him with love and patience. To-night at four he will die, I must be away now, but I hope to see him again before he dies."

Having thus spoken, alone and, contrary to his custom, without any one to accompany him, he left the house. Cataldus, Alvira, and a servant in the house testified to having seen him in Naples in their house; the servant even testified that he entered through closed doors; whilst two fathers who were with him at Recale gave sworn testimony that St. Francis was with them at the very time he was seen and spoken to at Naples.

And when the hour foreseen by this great saint, in which death was to place his cold hand on the brow of Cataldus, was at hand, the couch of the dying was again blessed by his spirit; but Alvira did not on this occasion see him, but she saw the recognition that cast a beam of joy over the face of the dying man, and she heard the sweet accents of consolation the saint was permitted to impart.

CHAPTER XXVIII.

A VISION OF PURGATORY—A DEAR ONE SAVED.

LIKE lengthening shadows of evening creeping over the silent ruin, death was fast drawing the shades of its final night over the austerities and the virtues of Alvira. The promises of St. Francis filled her heart with a cup of joy that rarely falls to the lot of mortals this side the grave.

Vespers are finished at the Gesù; the organ is silent, the crowd have departed, and, in the mellow twilight of an autumn eve, we discern only a few pious souls crouched behind the pillars, or pouring forth their last fervent aspirations before some favorite altar or saintly shrine. Soon all have left, and the silence of the abandoned sanctuary shrouds the fabric in greater solemnity. The aromatic incense still floats in nebulous veils around the tabernacle.

A loud breathing, an expression of joy from a dark recess, announced the presence of some one still in the church. The sounds came from the quarter known to the pious frequenters of the church as Magdalen's corner, so named because there was near to it an altar dedicated to the great penitent St. Magdalen, and because here St. Francis' Magdalen spent long hours in tears and prayer. On the evening in question Alvira had remained longer than usual to commune with Almighty God. It was a festival day, and her soul felt all the glow of fervor and spiritual joy which at times wraps the pious spirit into foretastes of celestial happiness. The hours passed swiftly by, for fervent prayer is not tedious to the loving.

She pondered in her mind what could be the graces or favors promised her in the last interview with her spiritual director. Her humility had not dared to seek favors; she was still overwhelmed with the thought of the bitter past; more time for repentance would be the signal favor she would venture to solicit from the God she had so much offended.

Yet the mercy and goodness of God are more mysterious to us mortals when we consider them lavished in extraordinary munificence on the souls of poor sinners. When we feel crushed to the earth in our unworthiness, the forgiving spirit of God lifts us up and pours around us consolations which are the privilege of the innocent. Thus the humble Alvira little dreamt what might be the grand consolations destined for her; but the time of their fulfilment has come, and we find her startled from an ecstasy in the church in which one of the promised favors was bestowed on this child of grace. She described to Father Francis what happened with many tears of joy.

Whilst wrapt in prayer in the lonely moments that followed the Benediction of the Most Holy Sacrament and the closing of the church doors, she suddenly saw the altar and sanctuary disappear, and in their stead a luminous bank of moving clouds;

they were white as the snow-drift, and crystallized in a flood of light like Alpine peaks in the winter sunshine

These clouds moved rapidly before her astonished gaze; occasionally she saw through their rents a tinge of red flame that glowed in the fleecy mist like the crimson linings of the sunset. The brighter clouds gradually faded; the flames became fiercer and more distinct; they seemed to leap in fury around the altar and sanctuary. Alvira struggled in doubt for a moment. Perhaps a real conflagration was consuming the tabernacle. A scream of agony was already on her lips, when the scene glided into a still more vivid reality, leaving no doubt as to its character. In the burning element human beings appeared writhing in pain; angels of dazzling brightness floated over the fire, and every moment caught the outstretched arms of some fortunate soul whose purgatorial probation had terminated; the angel would carry the soul to a distant sphere of brightness whither Alvira's weak mortal gaze could not follow.

Suddenly there darted from the far light an angel clothed with the brilliancy of the sun. With the speed of lightning he plunged far down the purgatory of fire; his brightness was so great that Alvira could follow him even through the flames. There the angel found a young, beautiful soul, deep in agony, clothed with crimson fire. A smile of ineffable joy lit up the countenance of the sufferer—the message from heaven was understood. The angel lifted this soul from the fire, and, pausing for a moment on the peak of a lambent flame, the angelic deliverer and the liberated soul, now become angelic in brilliancy, paused to look and smile on Alvira.

Her heart leaped, her soul trembled. She recognized the features. In a convulsive effort to utter the loved name of Aloysia, the vision passed away, and she found herself in the dark church and on the cold flags, weeping away the overflow of a heart too full of joy.

CHAPTER XXIX.

UNEXPECTED MEETING.

LATE on a cold night in the winter of 1706 a sick-call came to the Jesuit college attached to the Gesù. Alvira Cassier was ill, and requested the attendance of one of the fathers.

Some months had passed since the consoling vision in which she saw the purified soul of Aloysia carried to a crown of immortal bliss. Since then the great St. Francis had passed to his crown. His holy spirit hovered in protecting love over Alvira. She recurred to him in her troubles, and always with remarkable success. Miracles of cures and conversions, effected through the humble prayers of the penitent and the powerful intercession of the deceased apostle, are registered in the great book of life, to be read on the great accounting-day.

Alvira sighed over the prolongation of her exile. Her heart longed to be with Christ; she soared in spirit over the abyss that separated her from the object she loved.

Yet two more signs were to announce the happy moment of freedom. She knew the fate of Aloysia, raised from the searching flame and introduced to the saints, was the first of these favors promised by St. Francis. The other was equally extraordinary.

The illness of Alvira caused a sigh of regret at the Jesuit College. Every one whose heart was interested in the glory of God would have reason to sigh over her lost example, her influence over sinners, and the edification of her exalted virtues.

A priest is wrapped in his cloak; he carries the most Holy Sacrament and the holy oils. A levite accompanies him, carrying a lamp and ringing a bell. Unmindful of the inclemency of the weather, they move on through the abandoned streets, now filled by crowds of unseen angels, who take the place of man and honor the Holy of Holies.

The priest is a young Frenchman who has just come to Naples. To confer a favor on Alvira, the superior sent him to St. Francis's penitent that she might have the consolation of her own language at the trying hour of death. He is a tall, thin figure on the decline of manhood; in the graceful outline of features sweet and attractive we read the marks of much mortification. A halo of religion and sanctity envelopes him with that reverential awe we give to true virtue.

He has entered the room. Alvira starts.

She has seen that face before; that noble brow; that lofty mien; that irresistible sweetness of look. He is some acquaintance, perhaps met casual'y in the rambles of youthful folly. Reverence for the Blessed Sacrament banished further curiosity, and Alvira, with closed eyes and hands folded on her crucifix, joined in the solemn prayers recited on such occasions.

When all the prescribed ceremonies were completed, the good priest drew near the couch of the suffering invalid, and, allowing a moment for a relaxation of thought and for conversation, mildly enquired if she suffered much pain.

"So they tell me you have come from Paris, my child," we fancy we hear the good father commencing a conversation that leads to a strange discovery.

"Yes, father, 'tis my native city."

"And what was your family name?"

"Cassier."

"Cassier!" replied the priest, with a thrill of surprise. "Did he live in Rue de Seine?"

"Yes, father."

"You had a sister?"

"Yes; but she is now in heaven. She was killed on Mount Vesuvius." Alvira wept.

A startling suspicion had crept over the good priest. Was it possible that the invalid sinking into eternity in a sunset of sanctity and of heroic penance, formerly the chivalrous captain of Vesuvian fame, was no other than his own sister?

"And what became of your brother?" asked the Jesuit after a pause, and looking anxiously into Alvira's emaciated countenance.

"Ah! father," she replied, "I would give worlds to know. About thirty years ago, when our home was comfortable, he suddenly disappeared from us; no one could tell what became of him; we knew he was called by God to a holy life, and it was our impression at the time he fled to join some strict religious order. Poor dear Aloysia and myself used to pain him by turning his pious intentions to ridicule. His disappearance broke my poor mother's heart, for she died very soon afterwards."

A long, deep silence ensued. Père Augustin—for that was his name in religion—held his hands clasped up at his lips whilst Alvira was speaking. He remained motionless; his eyes were fixed on a spot on the floor. It was evident a struggle was going on within him. There could be no longer any doubt, and he was puzzled whether he should declare himself at once to be the lost Louis Marie, or bide his time and break it gently to her. As if seeking more time for deliberation, he asked her another question: "And, my child, what became of your father?"

Ah! how little did he dream of the wound he was tearing open. His enquiry was the signal for a new burst of grief from the broken-hearted Alvira. She buried her face in the pillow and wept violently. She remained so for several minutes. This made Père Augustin determine his course of action. As he had caused her so much pain, he must now console her by letting her know who he is. Drawing nearer to her, he bade her be consoled, for he had some good news to give her; and Alvira, after a great effort, raised her head and said:

"It is kind of you, father, very kind of you indeed, to take interest in my affairs;

but perhaps, as you are acquainted with Paris and belong to the Society of Jesus, you may know something of my brother. Poor Louis Marie! I should like to know if he is well, and happy, and good. Do tell me me, father, if you know anything of him."

"Yes, I do," answered the father quickly.

"Is he alive?"

"Yes!"

"And happy?"

"Yes."

"Where is he?"

"Here!" cried Louis Marie, bursting into tears—"here, within the grasp of your hand."

Could joy be greater? Those two holy souls blended into one. Like Benedict and Scholastica, they wept and smiled together in alternate raptures of joy and grief.

CHAPTER XXX.

CONCLUSION.

Now reft of all, faint, feeble, prest with age,
We mark her feelings in the last great stage;
The feverish hopes, the fears, the cares of life,
No more oppress her with torturing strife;
The chivalrous spirit of her early day
Has passed with beauty and with youth away.
As oft the traveller who beholds the sun
Sinking before him ere yet his journey's done,
Regrets in vain to lose its noontide power,
Yet hails the coolness of the evening hour,
She feels a holy and divine repose
Rest on her spirit in the twilight close;
Although her passions ruled in their might,
Now vanquished, brighter burns the inward light,
Guiding the spirit by its sacred ray
To cast its mortal coil and cares away,
And list its summons to eternal day.

Tossed on a restless ocean, and surviving a long and stormy voyage, how the sight of the verdant hills and the spires of the nearing port must cheer the wearied mariner! Joy has its sunbeams to light up every countenance. Merry the song that keeps tune with the revolving capstan. Old memories are awakened and dormant affections roused; the husband, the father, the exile, each has a train of thought laden with bright anticipations. Fancy and hope hasten to wave their magic wings over the elated heart, and contribute the balm of ideal charms to make even one moment of mortal life a happiness without alloy.

The wearied mariner returning home, quaffing a cup of joy, is a faint but truthful simile to represent the pious soul in sight of the port of eternal bliss, where loved ones are hailing from afar their welcome to the successful mariner from the troubled sea of time. Life has its storms and its calms, its casualties and dangers; it also has the bright twilight in the shadow of those eternal hills where existence is immortal and joy beatific and unclouded.

Alvira, the heroine of our sketch, is now

the faithful soul standing on the bark in view of her eternal home.

The consolations promised by her sainted guardian have twice tolled the death-knell; once more some great joy will strike the last fibre of a heart long tuned to spiritual happiness, and will break the last chain that imprisons a spirit longing to soar on high.

In the deceptive phases of the consumptive malady she rallied at times; she felt stronger—would venture out to the homes of the poor, and faint at the altar of Jesus. In her weakness she did not moderate her austerities, save where the express command of her spiritual director manifested to her the will of God. Her little cottage was surrounded daily by the poor and sick, who were her friends, and many and sincere were the blessings invoked over their benefactress.

Long and interesting were her conversations with her brother Louis. Her history as known to herself must have been replete with many striking events besides those we have caught up from a scanty tradition and a brief pamphlet biography. How the secrets of her rambles in disguise must have brought the smile and the blush to the countenance of her simple-minded and sainted brother!

In deep and natural fraternal affection, which is more powerful when mellowed by virtue, Père Augustin saw the hand of death making each day new traces on the frame of Alvira. The hectic flush, the frequent faintings, and the cold, icy grasp of her hand told the energy of the poison that gnawed at the vital cords. Sweet and gentle words of encouragement ever flowed from his lips. With eye and finger ever turning towards heaven, whither his own soul yearned, he calmed the anxious and penitent spirit of Alvira, who still feared her repentance imcomplete.

She received Holy Communion every day from the hands of her brother.

What ecstasies of grateful love filled her breast when preparing for those blissful moments of union with our Blessed Lord!

Deep and eloquent the mysterious breathings of the pure, loving heart. It has a language known and understood only by angels. As the sun melts the rocky iceberg, the coldest heart melts under the loving, burning Sun of the most Holy Eucharist.

At length the bark is anchored in the port of rest; Alvira is summoned to her crown.

The midnight of July 16, 1717, finds her in her agony; the blest candle is lighted; the faithful brother priest is kneeling by her bed; the solemn wail of the privileged few of the grateful poor is carried in mournful cadence from the chamber of death.

Yet the bell has not tolled the third stroke of consolation. Could she have misunderstood the prophetic voice of her sainted Father Francis, who knew the secrets of God in her behalf? But no; the favor will come—the last crowning, ineffable favor will come; it is at hand.

Alvira has opened her eyes. She calls

her brother near; with a smile, the sweetest that ever lit up those expressive features, she told him what the favor would be. Father Francis and the Blessed Virgin would see her before she should die.

Père Augustin believes the shock of approaching dissolution has weakened her reasoning faculty; he gently chides her, whispers some sweet thought of humility, and breathes the holy name that banishes temptation.

But, lo! Alvira's features have changed; a glow of ecstatic beauty has suffused around her; the light of another land is shed on her couch. Recognition is read on her looks.

Père Augustin, whose innocence and virtue entitled him to understand the privileges of the saints, saw the splendor of a heavenly light that filled the room, and heard from Alvira's lips expressions that left no doubt on his mind of the promised visit of celestial beings.

The light faded, and from the feeble glare of the candle of death he saw the holy spirit of his sister had fled; the sweetness of heavenly joy still played on her marble features, and the smile that greeted the heavenly visitors still rested on her lips.

Père Augustin stood over the couch he had bedewed with tears, and taking a long and affectionate glance at the hallowed form of his repentant sister, turned towards the weeping people; he raised his hand towards heaven, and solemnly announced the event that gave a festival to the angels. His voice faltered; he pronounced a short and eloquent panegyric—"A saint is dead!"

The tableau is worth remembering; 'tis the last beautiful scene in the eventful career of Maria Alvira Cassier!

THE END.

www.ingramcontent.com/pod-product-compliance
Lightning Source LLC
Chambersburg PA
CBHW021828230426
43669CB00008B/899